Read Me First

- Descriptions in this manual are based on what is available as at the time of writing this guide, and it may not be 100% accurate again if there is a significant software update to Fire HD Tablets 2019 Editions.

- All information supplied in this guide is for educational purpose only, and users bear the responsibility for using it.

- Although we took tremendous efforts to ensure that all information provided in this guide is correct, we will welcome your suggestions if you find out that any information contained in this guide is inadequate or you find a better way of doing some of the actions mentioned in this guide. All correspondence should be sent to **ajadirid1@gmail.com** or pharmibrahimguides@gmail.com

About This Guide

This is a very thorough, no-nonsense guide, useful for both experts and newbies.

Also including a bonus chapter:

- *An extensive guide on Alexa*
- *How to sideload apps (including Google Play store) on Fire tablets.*

This is a very detailed and extensive guide on Fire HD Tablets 2019 Editions. It is full of actionable steps, hints, notes, screenshots, and suggestions. This guide is particularly useful for newbies and seniors; nevertheless we strongly believe that even the techy guys will find benefits reading it.

Enjoy yourself as you go through this very comprehensive guide.

PS: Please make sure you don't give the gift of Fire HD Tablet 2019 Edition without giving this companion guide alongside with it. This guide makes your gift a complete one.

Table of Contents

How to Use This Guide

This guide is an unofficial manual of Fire HD Tablets 2019 Edition, and it should be used just like you use any reference book or manual.

To quickly find a topic, please use the table of contents. In addition, you use the index found at the back of this manual to search for information.

Lastly, when you are asked to tap a switch next to an item, just tap the box containing the switch. The switch should become colored when it is **On** (enabled).

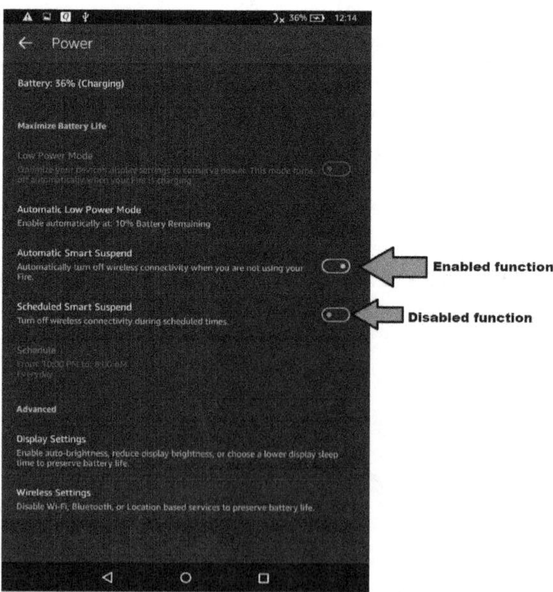

I hope this guide helps you get the most out of your Fire tablet.

Getting Started With Your Tablet

Unpacking Your Device

When you unpack your product box, check your product box for the following items:

1. Fire 7, Fire HD 8 or Fire HD 10 tablet (Depending on the one you purchase)
2. USB 2.0 charging cable and 5W/9W power adapter
3. Quick Start Guide

Hint: To charge your tablet in a faster manner, get a *9W Power adapter* made by Amazon (if not already included in the product box). This adapter will charge your tablet in an accelerated manner.

Turning your Tablet on and off

To turn on your tablet, press and hold the Power Key. If you turn on your tablet for the first time, follow the on-screen instructions to set it up.

To turn off your tablet, press and hold the power key and select **OK.**

To force Fire HD to shut down, press the power button until the tablet goes off. Please note that you may need to press and hold the power button of your device for up to 15 seconds before it turns off.

Note: It is advisable to charge your tablet before you set it up. However, if your device is fully charged when you received it, you may not need to charge it before using it. When your device is charging, you will see this icon  at the top right corner of the screen.

In addition, using another power adapter (other than the one that came with it) to charge your device may increase charging time. If you need to use another charger to charge your tablet, then consider these recommended chargers at http://pharmibrahim.blogspot.com/2015/10/blog-post.html.

Hint:

When you start using your Fire HD tablet, you may probably notice that its screen locks within a few seconds after you finish interacting with it. To allow the screen to stay longer before it locks, change the screen timeout setting. To do this:

1. Swipe down from the top of the screen and select settings icon
.

2. Tap **Display**.

3. Select **Display Sleep**. Then choose an option.

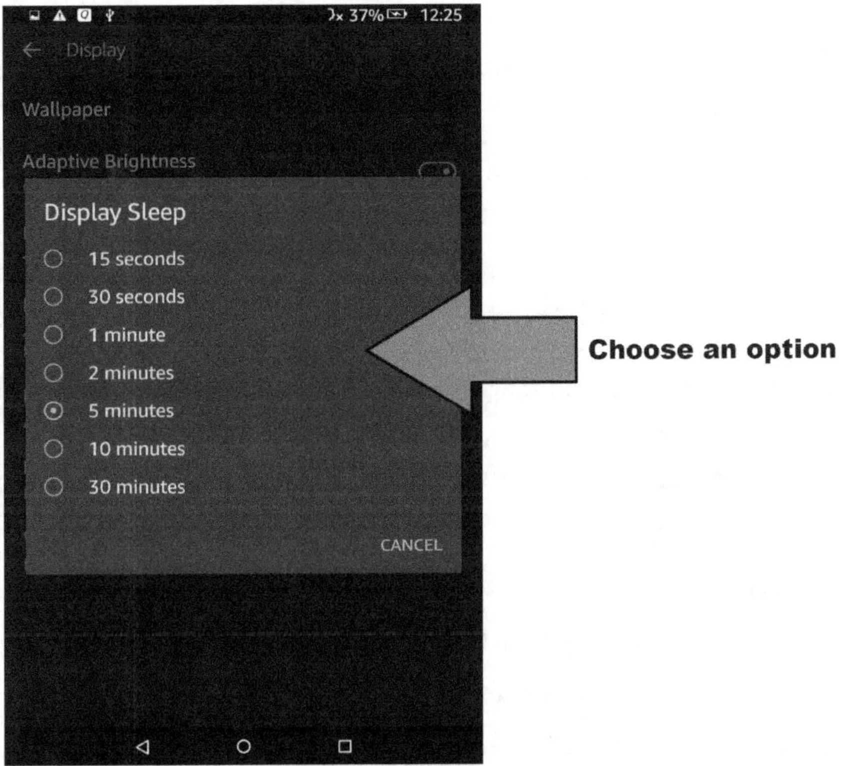

Please note that selecting a longer timeout may make your battery discharge faster.

Inserting and Managing SD Card

Fire tablet supports the use of external memory card and you can add a MicroSD card for up to 256GB - 512 GB.

Inserting a memory card

1. Hold your tablet making sure the front camera is facing you and the power button is up.

2. Gently open the SD card slot on your device.

3. Hold your memory card and make sure that the metal surface is facing up.

4. Gently slide in the memory card and make sure it fits in.

Removing the SD card

1. Swipe down from the top of the screen and select settings icon.

2. Tap **Storage.**

3. Scroll down and tap **Safely Remove SD Card** and then tap **OK**. Note that "Safely Remove SD Card" option might be unavailable when your tablet is connected to a PC.

4. Gently open the SD Card slot and then gently press the SD Card to remove it. Close the SD Card slot when you are done.

Hint: Please note that if you unmount the memory card without removing it from your device, you would need to mount it before it can be accessed again. To mount your memory card, follow the steps one and two above and tap **Mount SD Card**.

Managing Your SD Card

You can control how your device uses your SD Card.

To turn off the SD Card support for a particular content category (such as books):

Please note that this feature is turned on for all supported categories by default.

1. Swipe down from the top of the screen and tap settings icon 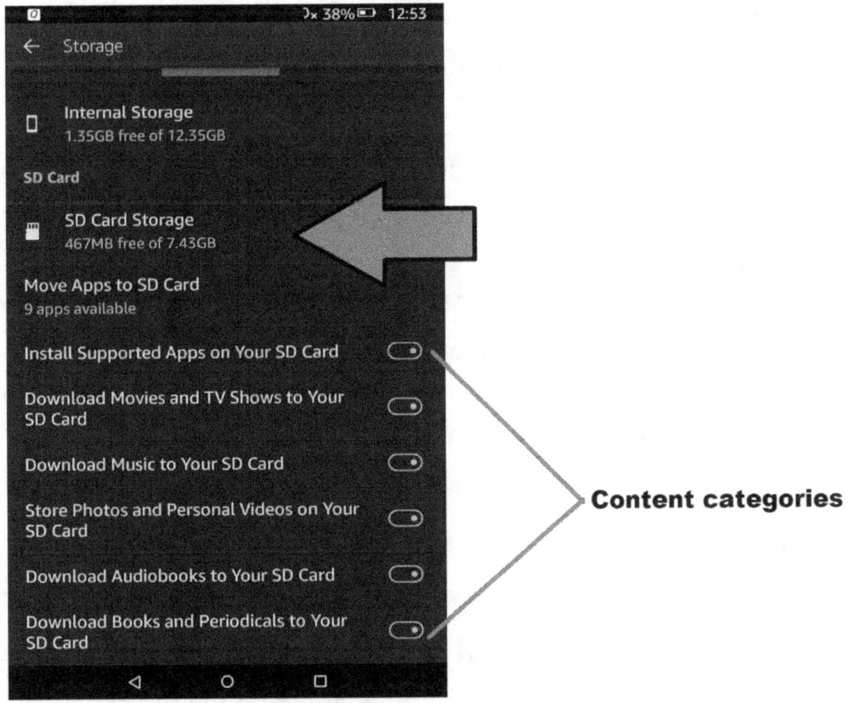, and then tap **Storage**.

2. Under SD card, tap a switch next to a content category to turn off the MicroSD card support for that content category.

3. To manage a particular content stored on SD Card, tap on **SD Card Storage** and then tap on the content you want to manage.

Notes:

1. Unless you disable the feature, all supported apps are automatically installed on your SD Card. In addition, downloaded video files and photos and videos taken with the camera will also be saved on your SD Card unless you disable the feature.

2. If you have multiple profiles on your device, videos downloaded to the MicroSD Card may only be available to the profile that downloaded it. In addition, photos and personal videos stored on SD Card may only be available to the profile that stored them. However, photos and personal videos that are transferred to your Fire tablet via USB or that were previously downloaded to a MicroSD card (before the creation of multiple profiles) may be available to all adult profiles.

To transfer apps from internal storage to SD Card:

1. Swipe down from the top of the screen and tap **Settings**, and then tap **Apps & Games**.

2. Tap **Manage All Applications.**

3. Select the app you want to transfer

4. Tap **Move to SD Card**. If the "Move to SD Card" option appears grey or it is not shown, then the option is not available for the chosen app.

Using the touch screen

Your tablet's touch screen allows you to easily select items or perform functions.

Notes:

- Do not press the touch screen with sharp tools on the touch screen. Doing so may damage the touch screen or cause it to malfunction.
- Do not allow the touch screen to come into contact with other electrical appliances. This may cause the touch screen to malfunction.
- Do not allow the touch screen to come in contact with water. YOUR DEVICE IS NOT WATER RESISTANT. The touch screen may malfunction in humid conditions or when exposed to water.
- For optimal use of the screen, you may need to remove the screen protector before using it. However, a good screen protector should be fully compatible and usable with your device.

You may control your touch screen with the following actions:
Tap: Touch once with your finger to select or launch a menu, application, or option.
Tap and hold: Tap an item and hold it for more than a second to open a list of options.
Tap and drag: Tap and drag with your finger to move an item to a different location in the application grid/list.

Locking and Unlocking the Touch Screen

When you do not use the device for a specified period, your device turns off the touch screen and automatically locks the touch screen so as to prevent any unwanted device operations and also save battery. To manually lock the touch screen, press the power key once.

To unlock, turn on the screen by pressing the power key and then swipe to unlock. If you have already set a lock screen password, you will be prompted to enter the password.

Note: You can activate the screen lock feature to prevent unwanted access to your tablet, to learn more please refer to page 23.

Rotating the touch screen

Your tablet has a built-in motion sensor that detects its orientation. If you rotate the device, the interface will automatically rotate according to the orientation. If you rotate your device horizontally, your device will change to Landscape mode, and if you rotate your device vertically, your device will enter Portrait mode.

> **Activating and deactivating screen rotation**

You may disable or enable screen rotation by following these steps:

1. To disable screen rotation, swipe down from the top of the screen to bring out **Quick actions menu**.

2. Tap on **Auto-Rotate** [Auto-Rotate] (So that it becomes Portrait)

3. To activate, tap on **Portrait** (So that it **Auto-Rotate**).

Navigating Apps on the Fire HD tablet

You can navigate apps on your tablet using the left panel. The left panel gives you more information about what you are viewing. To bring out the left panel, swipe from the left edge of the screen. The left panel gives you the menu information of an app.

The Back Button

We are including the back button under the getting started chapter because you will be using this feature a lot. Whenever you are done with a setting or feature and you don't see the **Done** button, you should consider using the back button. It is a smart way to get out of a menu when you are stuck and don't know what next to tap. There are two buttons that serve the purpose of a back button on your device, and they are:

1. **The small triangular button**: This is a small triangular button [◁] located at the bottom of the screen (beside the home button). Usually, tapping on this icon will take you back to the previous page.

2. **The small arrow button**: In some app panes, you will find another button that can serve as a back button. This button is a small arrow-like button usually located at the upper left corner of the screen. Please note that not all app panes will display this button. In fact, you may find out that many app panes don't contain anything like this.

Tip: You may use any of the back buttons described above to get out of any page when you are done with the page and you can't see the done option.

Getting to Know Your Home screen

From your Home screen, you can search for items and access applications. Swipe your finger up or down to see different apps on the Home screen. You can also quickly organize similar apps by tapping and dragging one app on top of the other. In addition, you can move an app from one location to another on the Home screen by tapping and dragging it.

Home screen has two different portions:

1. **The search portion:** This displays a search bar on top of the app grid. You can use this search bar to quickly find an item.

2. **The app grid portion:** This displays all the available apps in grid format. New apps you download are automatically added to the app grid. Once added to the app grid, the app will remain there until you remove it by uninstalling it.

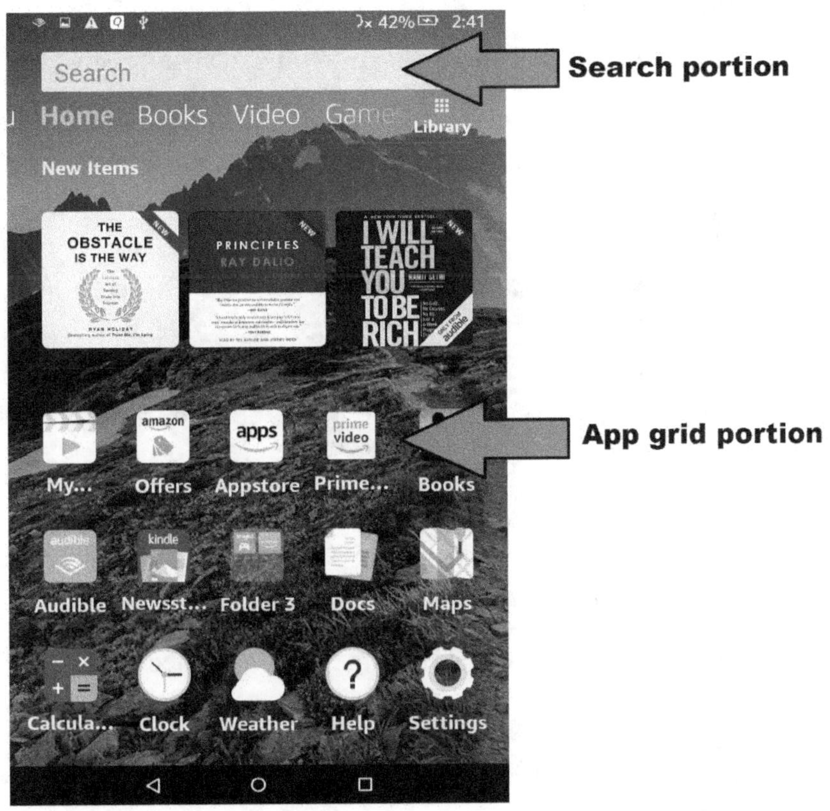

Removing items/apps from the Home screen

1. When on the home, tap and hold an item to open a list of options.

2. Select **Uninstall** found at the top of the screen.

3. Select **OK**.

Note: Selecting **Uninstall** will remove the app permanently from your device. In addition, Fire tablet comes preloaded with some apps and you may not be able to remove these preinstalled apps.

Home screen Categories

The Home screen has many categories and you can switch between them by swiping left or right. The categories include Books, Video, Games, Shop, etc. You can also switch between different categories by tapping on their name.

Please note that the present category bar would appear bold. For example, if the current category on your device is Home, it would appear bold. See the picture above.

When you are in a particular category page, you have access to two options, namely:

1. **Library**: This gives you access to all of your items.

2. **Store**: This gives you access to the Amazon store.

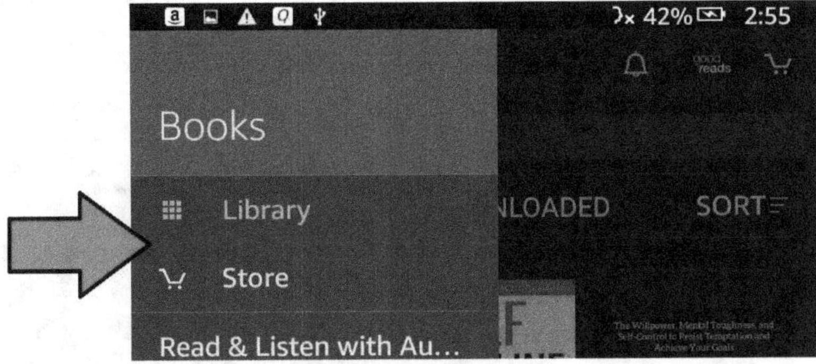

To Move an Item on the Application Grid Screen

1. Launch the application grid by tapping the Home screen button.

2. Tap and hold an item to move.

3. Drag the item to the location you want.

Create a folder of items/apps

1. From the Home screen, tap and hold an item, then drag and drop it directly on top of another item/app's icon to create a folder.

2. Then type in the folder name.

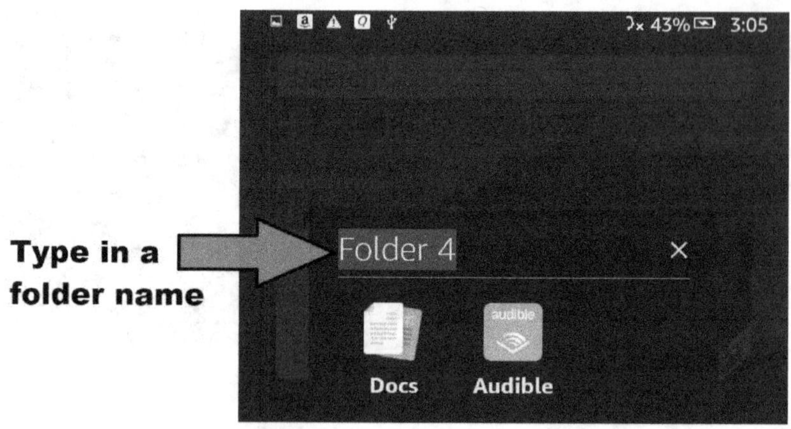

Removing apps from a folder

1. Open the folder you want to manage.

2. Tap and hold an app you want to remove, then drag it out of the folder.

3. Continue repeating step 2 above for all the apps you want to remove. When you remove the last app from the folder, the folder is automatically deleted.

Accessing Applications

1. Press the Home screen button to access the application grid.

2. Tap on the app of your choice.

3. To go back to the app grid screen, press the back button or the Home button (the buttons located at the bottom of the screen). If these buttons are not showing, tap the middle

of the screen or swipe up from the bottom of the screen to bring them to view.

Accessing Opened or Running Applications

1. Tap on the task-switcher button 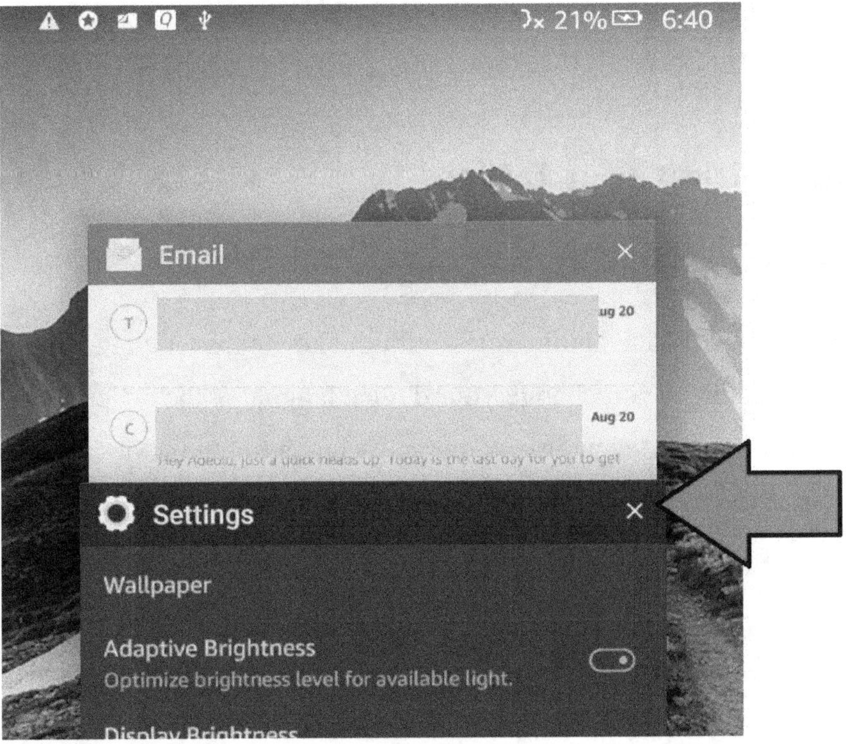 (the button beside the home button) to see all recently opened apps or items. This should contain all the opened/running apps.

2. Tap on the app to launch it, or tap on the **X** icon to close it.

Note: Although your tablet can run more than one app at the same time, multitasking may cause hang-ups, freezing, memory problems, or additional power consumption. To avoid these, end-all unused programs by closing the app.

Tip: You may consider installing app like **ES Task Manager** from the Amazon Appstore in order to better manage your apps. In addition, you can install **Files Go by Google** if you have installed Google Play on your tablet. To know how to install Google Play on your tablet, please go to page 190.

Customizing Your Tablet

Changing the device language

The device language is integrated with the keyboard language and this means that if you change your device language, the onscreen keyboard may also change automatically and assume the device language. See the next section to learn how to manually change your keyboard language.

If you are turning your tablet on for the first time, you should have the option to select a language of your choice. To change the language setting at any time, follow these steps:

1. Swipe down from the top of the screen to open the quick actions menu, and then tap **Settings** . Alternatively, you

may open the application grid and tap on the **Settings** icon

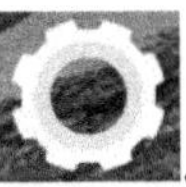.

2. Scroll down and tap on **Keyboard & Language.**

3. Tap on **Language**.

4. Tap the drop-down list and select a language from the list.

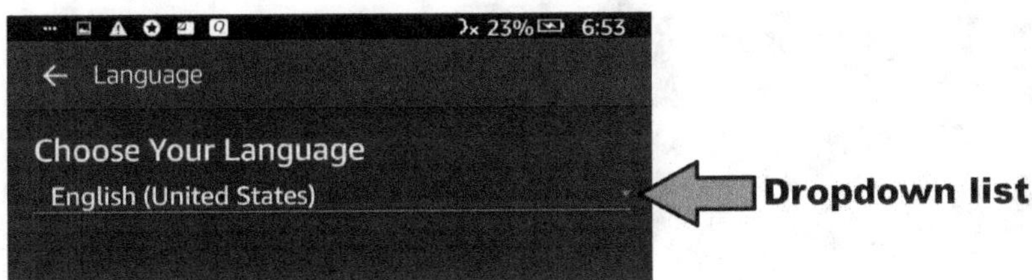

Changing the keyboard language

1. Swipe down from the top of the screen to open the quick actions menu, and then tap **Settings** .

2. Scroll down and tap on **Keyboard & Language**.

3. Tap on **Language** and select a Language. The keyboard may automatically assume the Language you choose for your device.

In addition, you can change the language of your keyboard without changing the language of your tablet. To do this:

1. Repeat steps 1 and 2 above.

2. Tap on **Show/Hide Keyboard**.

3. Enable the language you want to use. Press the back button to return to the previous page.

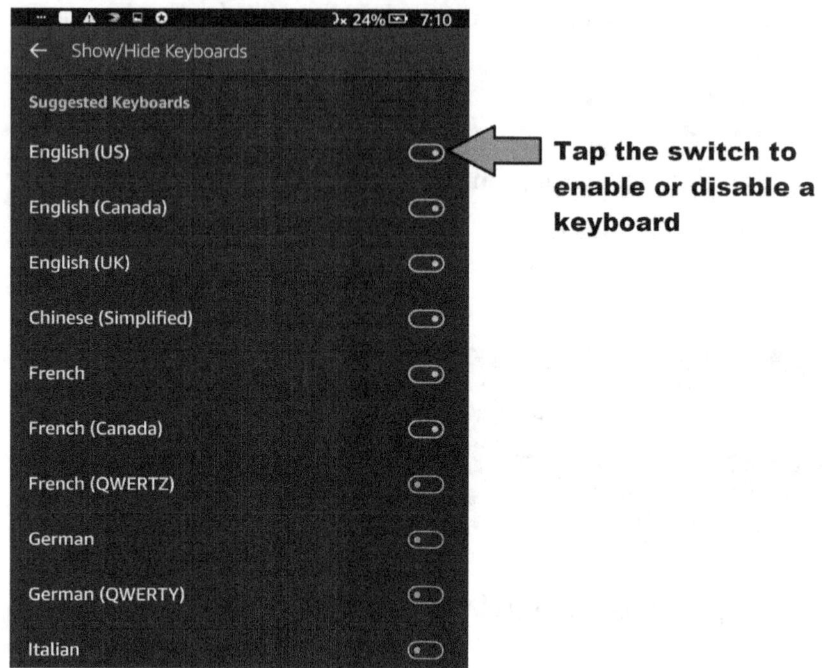

4. Then tap on **Current Keyboard** and choose a keyboard in your desired language.

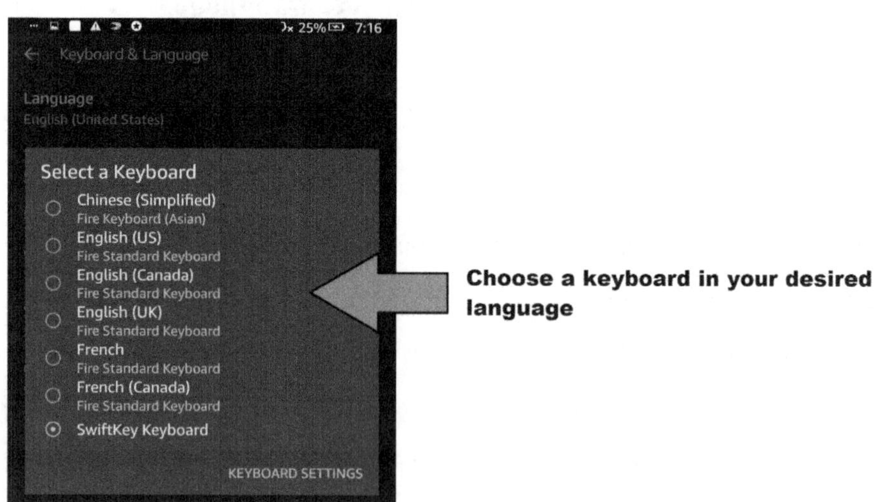

Tip:

You can manage the settings of your chosen keyboard by following
the steps below:

1. Swipe down from the top of the screen to open the quick
   actions menu, and then tap **Settings** .
2. Scroll down and tap on **Keyboard & Language**.
3. Tap **Current Keyboard Settings**.
4. Adjust the settings as you like.

Note: You can download a keyboard from Google Play Store. To
know how to install Google Play Store on your tablet, please go to
page 190.

Hint: To quickly change your keyboard language while using the
keyboard, long-press the virtual **Spacebar** on the keyboard and then
select the language of your choice.

Set the current time and date

Fire tablet automatically sets time based on time zone. To set the
time zone, perform the following actions.

1. Swipe down from the top of the screen to open the quick
   actions menu, and then tap **Settings** .
2. Tap on **Device Options**.
3. Then tap on **Date & Time**.
4. Make sure **Automatic Time Zone** is disabled.
5. Then tap on **Select Time Zone** and choose a time zone.

Managing notification and sounds options

1. Swipe down from the top of the screen to open the quick actions menu, and then tap **Settings** .
2. Scroll down and tap on **Sound & Notification**.
3. Tap on **Default Notification Sound** and select your preferred sound.
4. To manage how you see your notifications while your device is locked, tap on **When Device is Locked.**
5. To select which app can send you notifications, tap on **App Notifications** and choose an app. Then adjust the notification settings as needed.
6. To adjust the system and notification volume, adjust the slider next to **System & Notification Volume**.

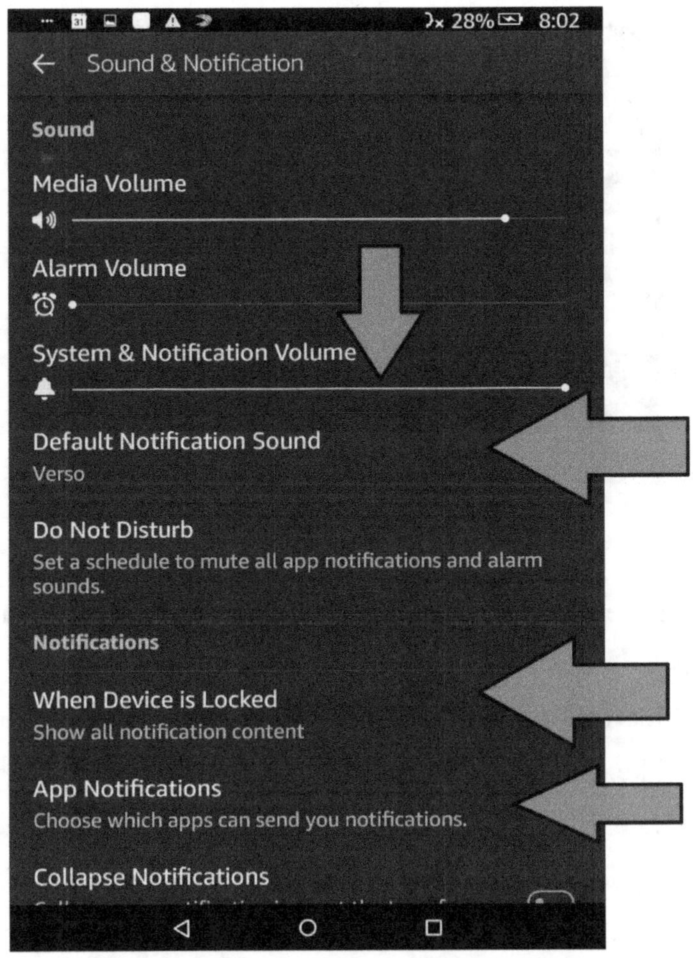

Hint: To completely mute your device if you don't want any distraction, swipe down from the top of the screen and tap **Do Not Disturb**.

In addition, to disable notification from an individual app, go to **Settings** > **Apps & Games** > **Manage All Applications**. Then tap an app and uncheck the box next to Show notifications.

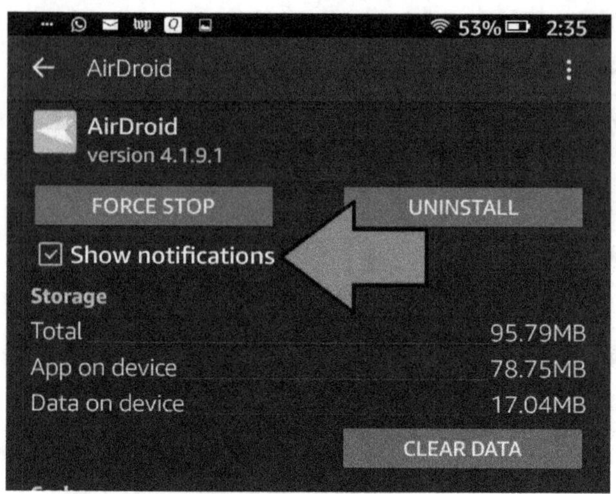

Adjusting the tablet's volume

1. Press the volume key up or down to bring up the volume panel.

2. Use the volume keys to adjust the volume of your tablet as you like.

3. To mute all sound, swipe down from the top of the screen to open quick actions menu and tap on **Do Not Disturb**. Please note that when **Do Not Disturb** is enabled, you would not be able to use the volume key to adjust the volume.

Adjusting the brightness of the display

1. Swipe down from the top of the screen to open the quick actions menu.

2. Drag the slider to adjust the brightness.

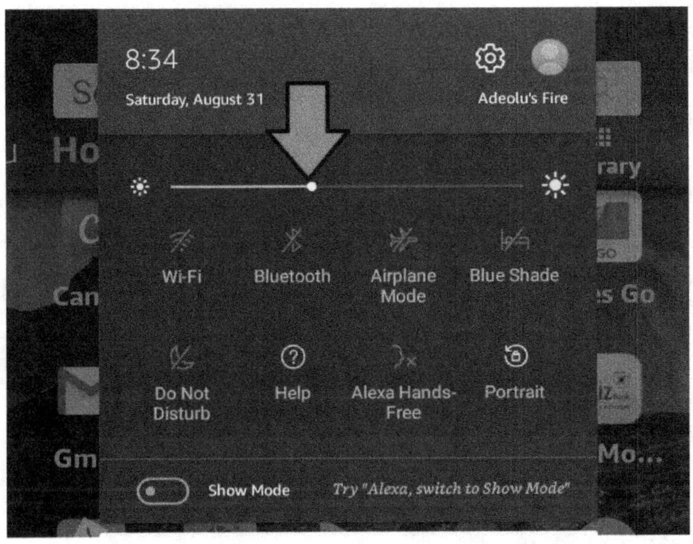

Hint: The brightness level of the display will affect how quickly the device consumes battery power. I will advise that you turn it reasonably low if you are very concerned about saving your battery.

Setting the screen lock password or PIN

You can lock your tablet by activating the screen lock feature.

Note: Once you set a screen lock, your tablet will require an unlock code each time you turn it on or unlock the touch screen.

1. Swipe down from the top of the screen to open the quick actions menu, and then tap **Settings** . Then scroll down and tap on **Security & Privacy**.

2. Tap the switch next to **Lock Screen Passcode.**

3. Tap **PIN** or **Password** and enter the **PIN/ Password** you like. Tap **Finish** when you are done.

Notes:

1. Setting a passcode is an excellent way to prevent unwanted access to your device. I will recommend that you use a password to lock your device instead of using a PIN. A password can combine letters, numbers, and special characters and therefore provides more security than a PIN.

2. If you plan to setup Amazon FreeTime profiles on your device, please note that the lock screen password/pin must be turned on. It is part of the requirements for setting up FreeTime profiles. To learn more about Amazon FreeTime, please go to page 102.

Hint: To view your recent notifications while the screen is locked, swipe down from the top of the screen. But you will need to unlock your device by entering your PIN/password (if you have any) to view your notifications details.

Setting a wallpaper

1. Swipe down from the top of the screen to open the quick actions menu, and then tap **Settings**.

2. Tap on **Display**.

3. Tap on **Wallpaper**.

4. Tap on **Pick image** found on the lower-left corner of the screen and pick an image.

Adjusting Font Size on Your Tablet

You can change the font on your tablet to a bigger or smaller font by following the steps below:

1. Swipe down from the top of the screen and tap settings icon 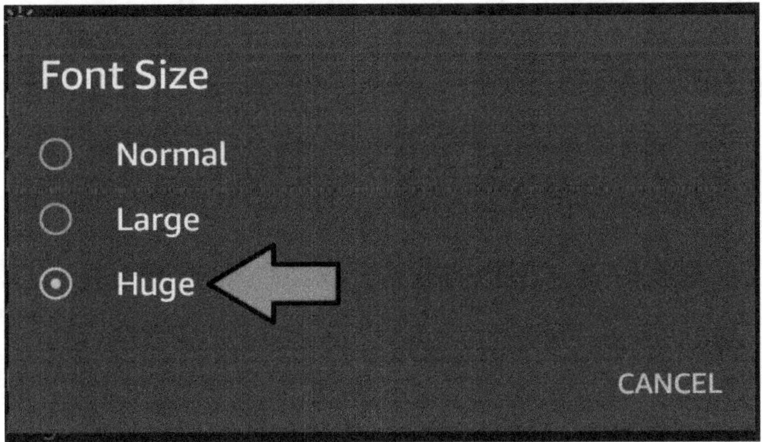.

2. Tap **Display**.

3. Select **Font size** and pick an option.

Tip: If you have a senior that has a problem understanding what is on the screen, you could increase the font size using the method above.

Uninstalling/Deleting an App

If you don't need an app again, you can uninstall it. To do this:

1. From the Home screen, locate the app you want to uninstall. Tap and hold this app for two seconds and lift your finger. Then select **Uninstall**.

2. Tap **OK** to confirm.

Note: Please note that you might not be able to uninstall some of the apps that come preloaded on your device.

Entering a text

You can enter text by selecting characters on the virtual keypad.

Note: You can change the writing language to anyone supported. For more information refer to page 17.

To enter text:

1. Enter text by selecting the corresponding alphabet or numbers.

2. You can use any of the following keys:

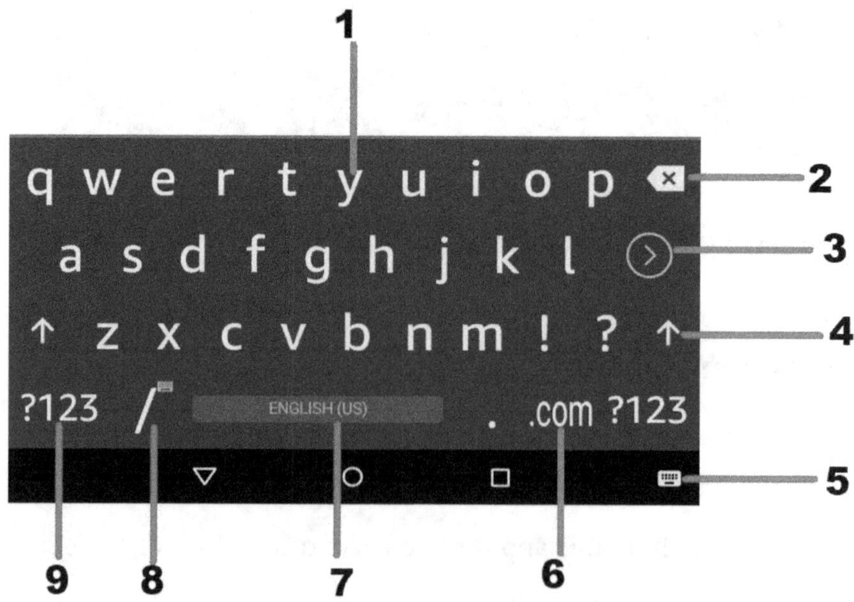

Number	Function
1.	Virtual keyboard alphabets
2.	Clear your input/backspace
3.	Tap this to start a new line, launch a webpage or go to another tab.
4.	Change case
5.	Tap this to change the keyboard type
6.	Tap this to insert .com. To enter other variants, tap and hold **.com** and choose an option.
7.	Spacebar. Tap this to insert a space. To quickly change your keyboard language while using the keyboard, long press this spacebar key and then select the language of your choice.
8.	Tap this once to insert / key. To split your keyboard into two, tap and hold on the slash (/) key.
9.	Switch between Number/Symbol and ABC mode. **Hint:** To return to ABC mode, tap on the **ABC** key located on the keyboard.

Tips:

When entering a web address, press and hold on the **.com** key to get access to other variants like .gov, .co.uk etc.

To copy and paste a text

While you are entering text, you can use the copy and paste feature.

1. Tap and hold a word, and drag   or   to select the text you want.

2. Then select "Copy" to copy, or select "Cut" to cut the text onto the clipboard.

3. In another application or where you want to place the text, tap and hold the text input field.

4. Then select "Paste" to insert the text from the clipboard into the text input field.

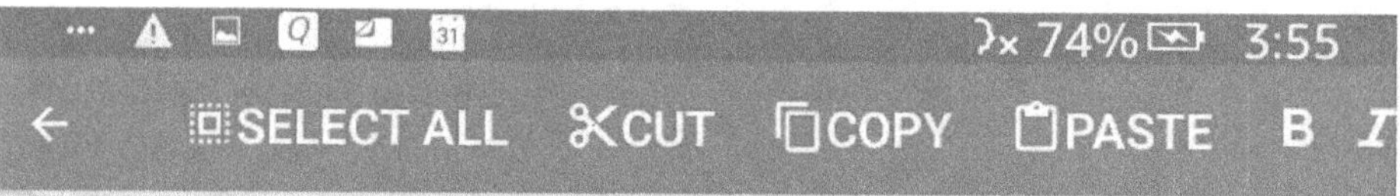

Airplane mode

In airplane mode, you can disable all wireless connections. This may be important in hospitals and airports. This feature also helps you save battery power.

1. Swipe down from the top of the screen to open the quick actions panel.

2. Tap on the **Airplane Mode** button.

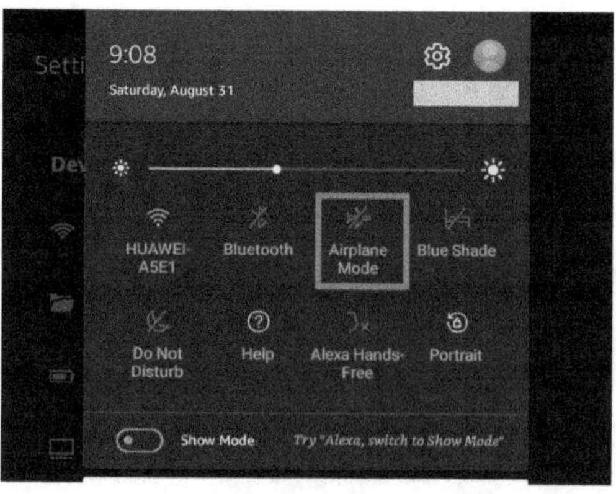

Using The Special Features

Fire tablets come with special features that differentiate them. Some of these features are discussed below.

Alexa

Alexa is a trained virtual assistant that has been built to answer questions. This section of the guide will show you how to manage Alexa like a pro and how to ask questions and give commands that Alexa will understand.

Disabling/Enabling Alexa

You can disable or enable Alexa by following the steps below:

1. Swipe down from the top of the screen to open the quick actions menu, and then tap **Settings** ⚙
2. Tap on **Alexa**.
3. Tap the switch next to **Alexa**.

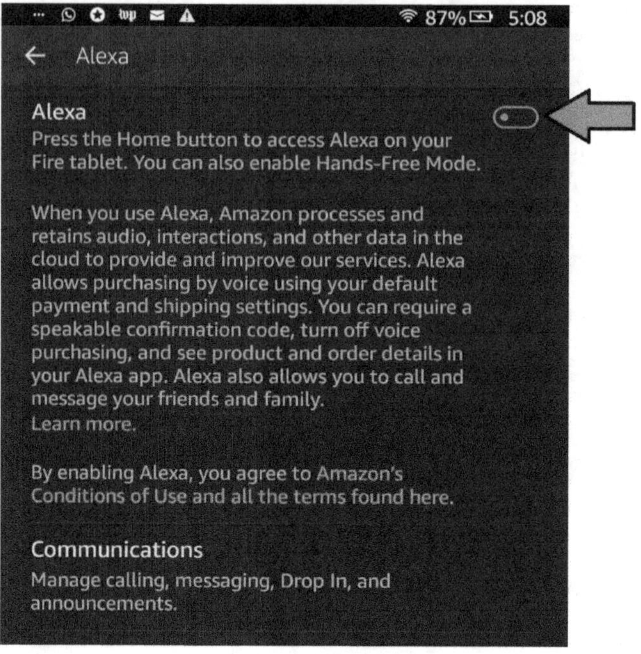

4. To disable Alexa, tap the status switch next to **Alexa**.

Speaking to Alexa

One of the ways you will interact with Alexa is by saying your questions. There are few things to know when talking to Alexa so as to get the best experience.

To get Alexa into action, you will need to get its attention. To do that, please follow the steps below:

1. Press and hold the Home button (the middle button at the lower part of the tablet) until you see a blue line at the bottom of the screen (you may also hear a tone).

2. Then speak your question to it. It will then give you an answer. If you want to ask another question, press and hold the Home button again.

To get Alexa to respond to your voice without pressing the Home button, do these:

1. Swipe down from the top of the screen to open the quick actions menu, and then tap **Settings**.
2. Tap on **Alexa**.
3. Tap the switch next to **Hands-Free Mode**.

Many times, Alexa will also display a card containing an answer in addition to the voice feedback. To dismiss this card, press the back button.

Change the Wake Word

To get the attention of Alexa you will need to say the wake word followed by the command.

Amazon allows you to choose between Alexa and Amazon

To change your wake word:

1. Swipe down from the top of the screen to open the quick actions menu, and then tap **Settings**.
2. Tap on **Alexa**.
3. Make sure **Hands-Free Mode** is enabled.
4. Tap on **Wake Word**.
5. Select **Amazon**.

Using Quick Commands (Routines) to Manage Alexa Like a Pro

Quick commands (routines) allow you to use Alexa in a special way. When you say a specific quick command, you trigger a set of actions from Alexa.

Examples of quick commands include:

a) Alexa start my day b) Alexa, good night c) Alexa, on my way d) Alexa, driving.

For example, if you say **Alexa, good night**, a set of actions (attached to Goodnight) are performed by Alexa.

To enable and manage quick commands (routines):

1.   Open Alexa app and tap on the menu icon located at the top left corner of the screen.

2.   Tap on **Routines**.

3.   Tap the plus (+) icon usually found at the top of the screen.

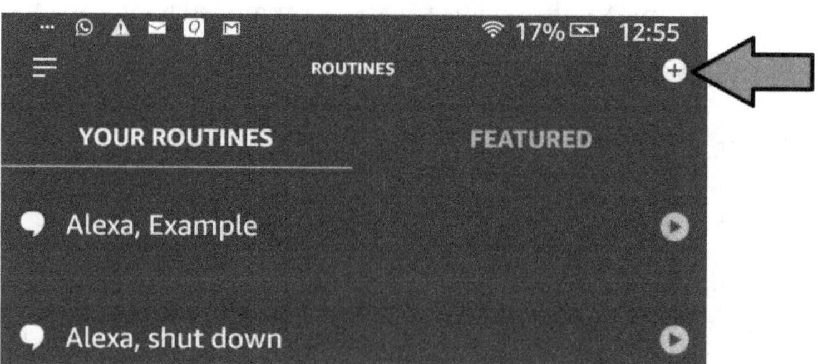

4. Tap **When this happens**. Then tap **Voice**. Type in an example command, for example, type in **Welcome me home**.

5. Tap **Save**

6. Tap **Add action**. Tap a category and select a sub-category if needed. Then select **Add**.

7. To add another action, select **Add action**. Tap a category and select a sub-category if needed. Then select **Add**. Repeat this step for all other actions you want to add.

8. To remove an action, tap the minus icon next to the action.

9. If available, select **The device you speak to** and pick **This mobile device**.

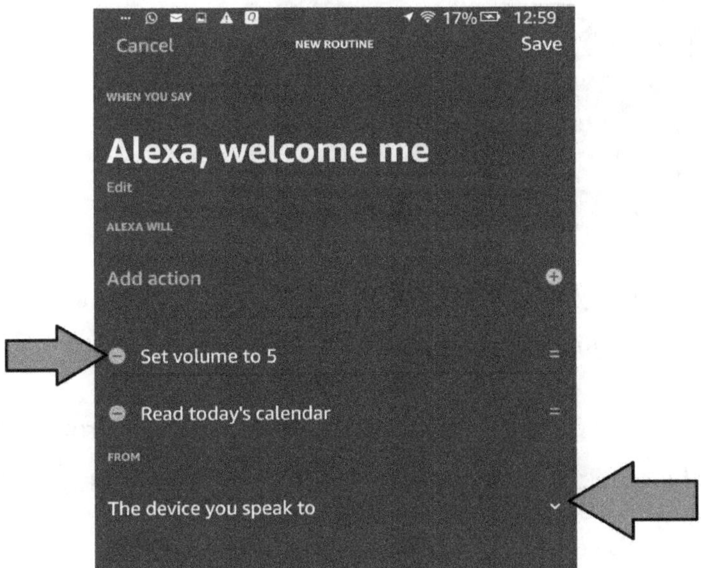

10. Tap **Save/Create** found at the top of the screen and wait for the process to finish.

11. To add more quick commands, tap the plus icon + at the top of the screen and repeat steps 4 to 8 above.

12. To delete a quick command (routine), tap the routine, and tap the menu icon located at the top of the screen. Then select **Delete Routine**.

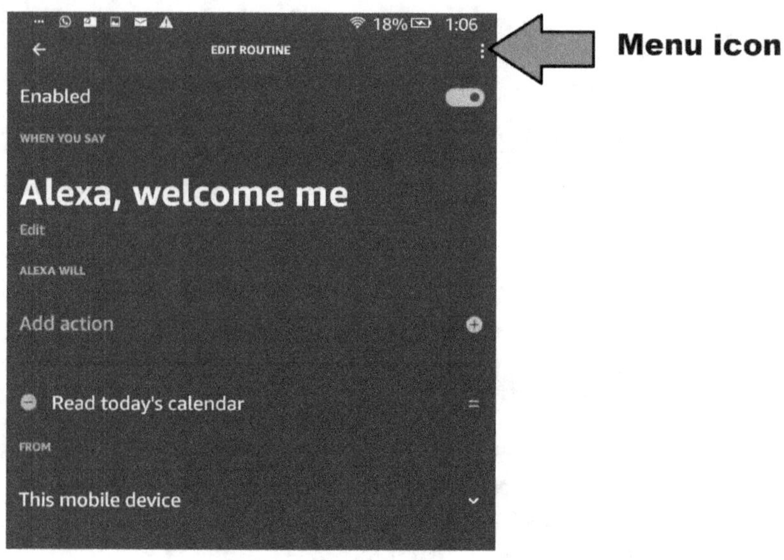

That is all! Now you can get Alexa to perform all the chosen actions by saying your quick command.

Tip: You could add more actions to a quick command/routine. To do this, tap the quick command/routine and select **Add action**. Then follow the prompts.

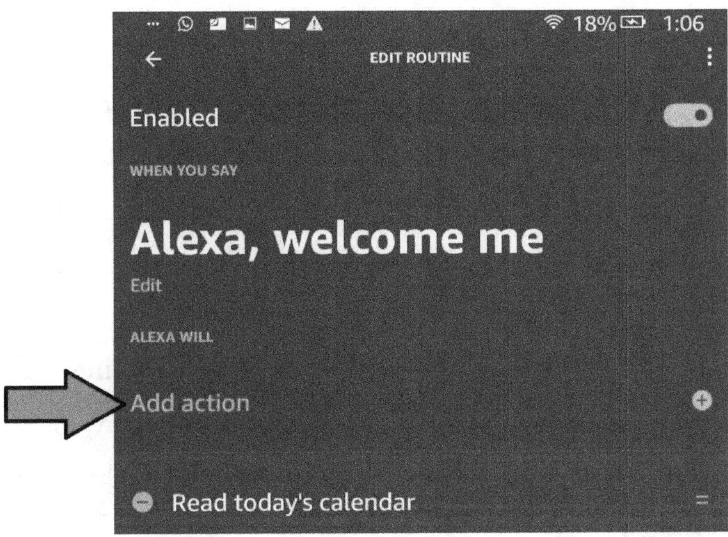

Using Alexa to Open Apps or Programs

One of those things you will want to use Alexa to do is access your apps. You can quickly open an app by pressing and holding the Home button and then saying **Open** followed by the app's name. For example, to open calculator, say **Open calculator**.

Using Alexa with Different Types of Skills

You can give a new set of skills to Alexa using the Alexa app. So, what is a skill? A skill is a special action performed by Alexa when it is connected to another device, app, website or item. For example, you can give Alexa some extra mathematical skills by connecting it to a third-party skill called **Math Puzzle.** In addition, you can give Alexa some flight information capabilities by connecting it to a third-party skill called **KAYAK.** Furthermore, you can give Alexa some smart control capabilities by connecting it to a skill called **SmartThings**.

In a nutshell, connecting a skill to Alexa transforms the way you use your Fire tablet. It lets you do what you can't do with Alexa alone. In this section of the guide, you will be learning the basic steps to follow to connect a new skill to Alexa.

To add a skill to Alexa:

1. Open Alexa app and tap on the menu icon located at the top left corner of the screen.
2. Tap on **Skills & Games.**
3. Tap on **Categories** and choose a category and then a skill you like. Alternatively, tap the search bar located at the top of the screen and enter a search phrase.
4. Tap a skill, read the skill descriptions and then tap **Enable To Use** to activate the opened skill. Please note that you may be required to enter some account information to fully enable a skill.
5. You are now ready to use the new skill.

Tip: To link a smart home device, just follow steps 1 to 3 above and tap on **Smart Home** category. Then choose a skill corresponding to the smart home device you are trying to use with Alexa. Tap **Enable To Use** and follow the prompts.

Please note that it is essential you read the skill description page to know how to manage a smart home skill/device.

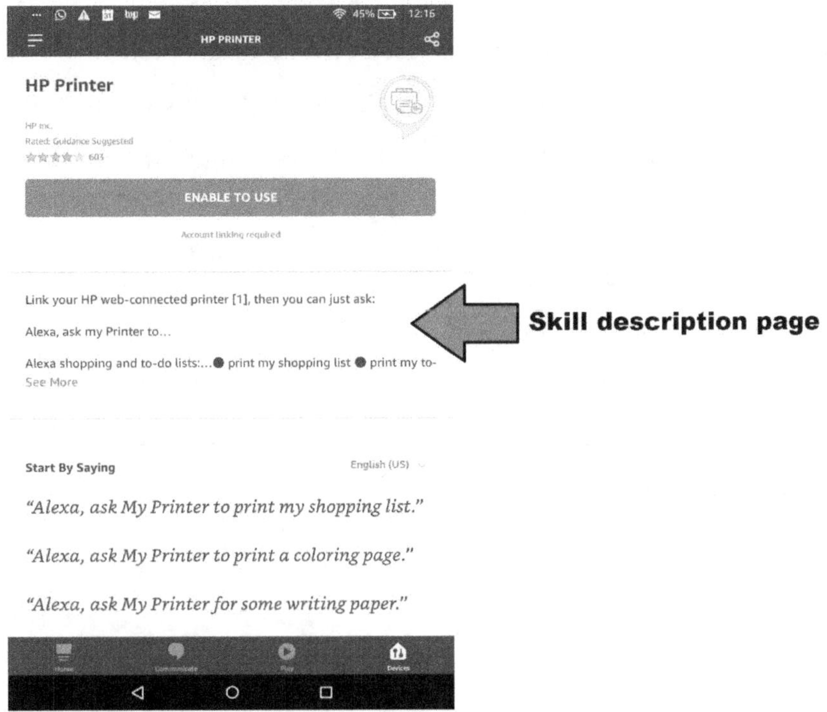

In addition, you may be able to enable/disable some skills using your voice (you have to say their exact name). For example, you may say:

- **Alexa, enable Kayak**
- **Alexa, disable Kayak**

Hint: Do you want to use Alexa in a special way? Then add nice skills to it. You can know how to use a skill by reading the information on the details page of the skill.

In addition, you can know the top skills on Amazon by saying, **Alexa, what are your top skills?**

Connecting Your Smart Devices to Alexa

You can link many smart home devices by following the steps mentioned on page 36. However, not all smart home devices may be linked by following the steps on page 36. If the method in the preceding section does not work, please try these:

1. Open Alexa app and tap on the menu icon located at the top left corner of the screen.
2. Tap on **Add Device**.
3. Select the device category or select the device from popular brands category.

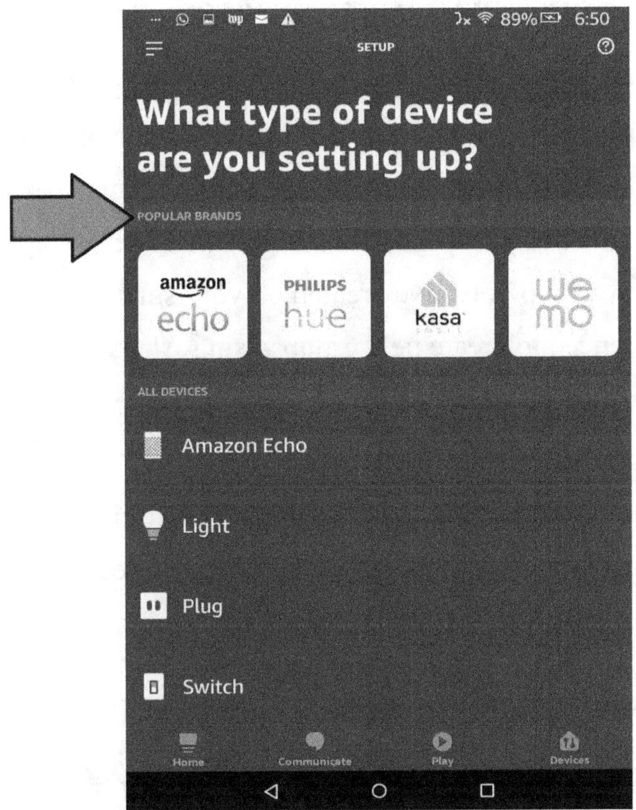

4. Carefully follow the onscreen instructions to complete the setup process.

Tip: If Alexa can't still discover your device after following the steps mentioned in this guide, check the companion app for your smart home device to ensure that it's on the same Wi-Fi network as your Alexa app.

In addition, please note that if you turn off or unplug your smart home device and then turn it back on, it may take some time before Alexa app can rediscover the device.

Grouping Your Smart Home Devices

Grouping your smart home devices allows you to control them smartly. For example, you can create a group and name it **bedroom light** so that Alexa can access them whenever you make a command and you include bedroom light. Please note that Alexa may not recognize any group you have created on your smart home device and you may need to create new groups using Alexa app.

To create a group:

1. Open Alexa app and tap on devices icon located at the bottom right corner of the screen.
2. Tap on the plus icon at the top of the screen.

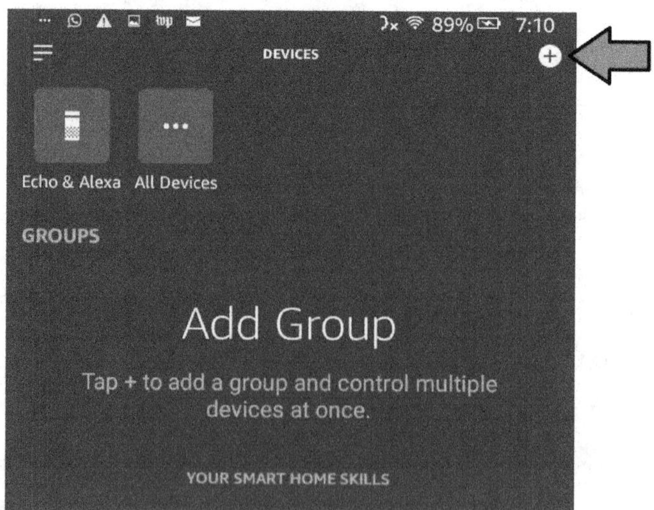

3. Select **Add Group**.
4. Enter the group name in the field provided or select a name from the list provided. If you are typing a name, make sure

you give your group a recognizable name for Alexa to identify. For example, you may use the name **Living Room light** to denote the light bulbs in your living room. Then select **Next**.

5. Select all the smart home devices you want to add by tapping each one of them. Then select **Save**.

To edit/manage a group:

1. Open Alexa app  and tap on the devices icon located at the bottom right corner of the screen.

2. Tap on the group you want to edit.

3. Tap **Edit** next to the group you want to edit.

4. To edit the name of your group, select **Edit Name** next to the group name.

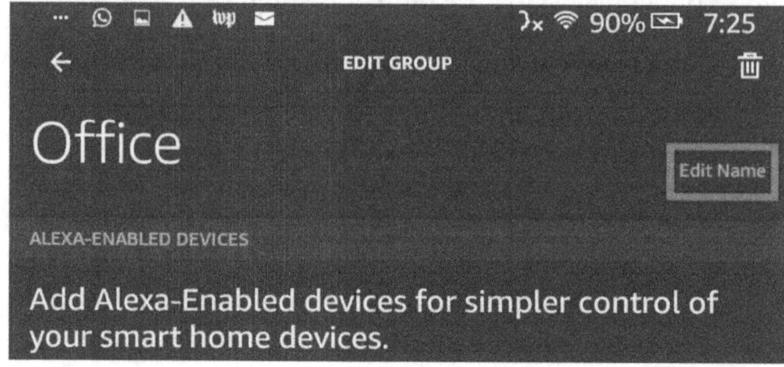

5. To add more smart home devices, simply select them. Tap **Save** (found at the bottom of the screen) to save the changes.

6. To delete a group, tap the delete icon located at the top of the screen.

Using Alexa with Smart Home Devices

You can use Alexa to control your smart home devices. This is particularly interesting; imagine telling Alexa to turn on/off the light with just a voice command.

We will assume that you have already connected your smart home devices to your Alexa using the instructions on page 38-39.

After connecting your smart home device to Alexa, press and hold the Home button until you see a blue line and then say the example commands found below. Alternatively, say **Alexa** followed by example commands below:

- Turn on/off (smart home device/group name). For example, you may say **Turn off bedroom light**.

- Brighten/dim (smart home device/group name). For example, you may say **Brighten my living room light.** You may also say **Set my living room light to maximum**.

- Set (smart home device/group name) temperature to (lower/higher) degrees. For example, you may say **Set Samsung thermostat to 20 degrees.**

- Set (smart home device/group name) to "x". For example, you may say **Set Living room fan to 5.**

Note: As I have said before, you will need to connect your smart home devices to Alexa before you can use Alexa to control these devices. To learn how to connect Alexa to your smart device, please go to page 38.

Using Alexa with Your Calendar

One of the fantastic features that Alexa can do for you is making an appointment.

With just a few commands, you can get Alexa to put an event or appointment into your calendar. But before you can populate your calendar with events, you will need to first link your calendar to your Alexa app. To do this:

1. Open Alexa app and tap on the menu icon located at the top left corner of the screen.
2. Tap on **Settings**.

3. Scroll down and select **Email & Calendar**.

4. Select **Add Account**.

5. Select an account type and carefully follow the onscreen instructions to complete the setup process.

6. To unlink your calendar at a future time, tap the account and select **Unlink account**.

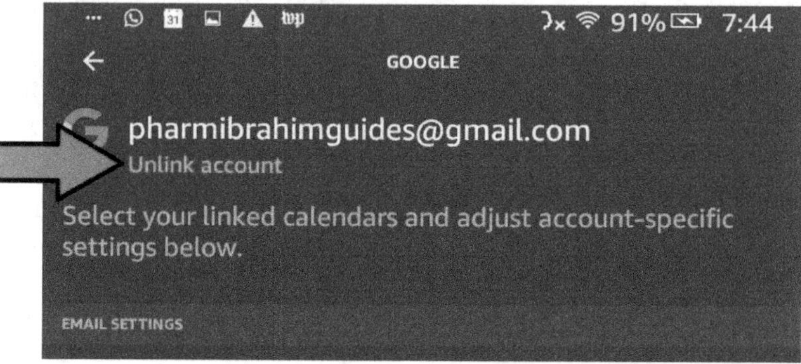

Note: *Please note that after adding your calendar/email account, content from your calendar and email may be available to anyone using your Alexa devices (i.e. Fire tablet) and will be stored in the cloud.*

After linking your Google Calendar to Alexa, tap and hold the Home button until you see a blue line or say **Alexa**. Then say things like:

- **What is on my calendar tomorrow?**

- **Add an event to my calendar.**

- **How does my calendar look like today**?

- **Add meeting with Clinton to my calendar for Friday at 6 a.m.**

- **Add an appointment with Steve for Monday at 1 p.m.**

Please note that you can also say all the examples given above in other ways, the most important thing is to get Alexa to understand what you are saying.

Using Alexa with Your Shopping List and To-do List

There are probably many things going through your mind and it will be quite interesting if you can get a personal assistant to assist in putting it down inside a list. Fortunately, Alexa can help you in this regard.

To add an item to your to-do list or shopping list, tap and hold the Home button until you see a blue line or say **Alexa**. Then say things like:

- **Add 'go to my in-law house' to my to-do list**

- **Add (item) to my shopping list**

- **What's on my shopping list**

- **What's on my to-do list?**

Tip: You can manage your shopping or to-do list using Alexa app

:

1. Open Alexa app 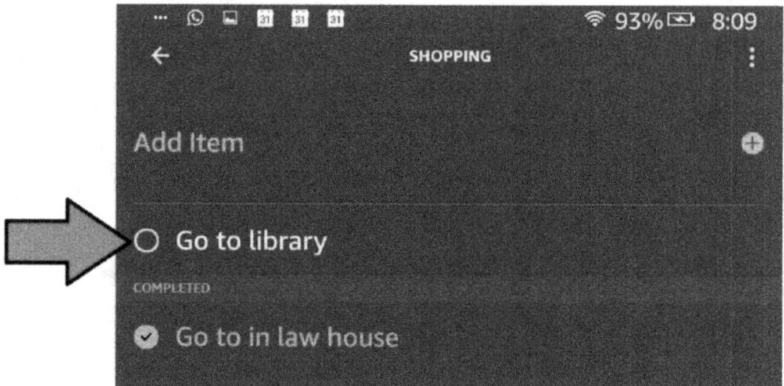 and tap on the menu icon
   located at the top left corner of the screen.

2. Tap on **Lists**.

3. Select **Shopping** or **To-do** list.

4. To add a new item to the list, tap the plus icon "+."

5. Type in what you want to do or buy into the **Add Item** field.

6. Tap on the arrow icon or the check mark on the virtual
   keyboard to save the changes.

7. When you are done with the list, select the circle next to the
   list to move it to **Completed** list category.

8. To delete or clear the completed items list, select three-dots
   icon (found at the top of the screen) and choose **Clear
   Completed**.

In addition, you can print your list if you are accessing Alexa app from a computer, to access Alexa app from a computer, go to http://alexa.amazon.com. Then in the left navigation menu, click **Lists.** Choose either list. Then select **Print** (found at the top right part of the screen).

Furthermore, you can link a third-party To-Do lists so that Alexa can make your Shopping List and To-do List available in third-party services. To do this:

1. Open Alexa app and tap on the menu icon located at the top left corner of the screen.
2. Tap on **Settings**.
3. Select **Lists**.
4. Tap on a third-party service and select **Enable to Use** (if available). Then carefully follow the on-screen instructions to finish the setup.

Using Alexa with Alarm

You can also set an alarm using this personal assistant. To do this, say **Alexa** followed by these example commands:

- **Set an alarm for 1 p.m. tomorrow**
- **Set an alarm for 30 minutes from now.**

Tip: To stop the alarm when it is sounding, say **Alexa, stop the alarm**. You may also say **Alexa, snooze the alarm.** This will snooze the alarm for a particular period of time.

To set a repeating alarm, tap and hold the Home button until you see a blue line or hear a sound. Then say:

- **Set an everyday alarm for 7 a.m.**

To know the status of your alarm, tap and hold the Home button until you see a blue line or say **Alexa**. Then say things like:

- **What time is my alarm set for?**
- **What alarms do I have for Monday?**

To edit/delete an alarm:

1. Open Alexa app 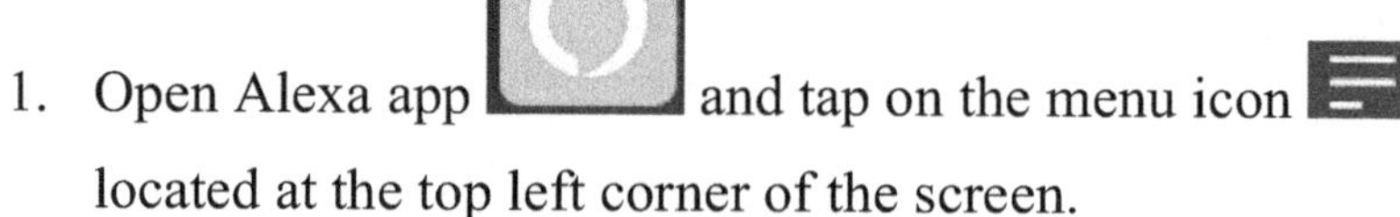 and tap on the menu icon located at the top left corner of the screen.
2. Tap on **Reminders & Alarms.**

3. Choose your device from the drop-down menu found at the top of the screen.

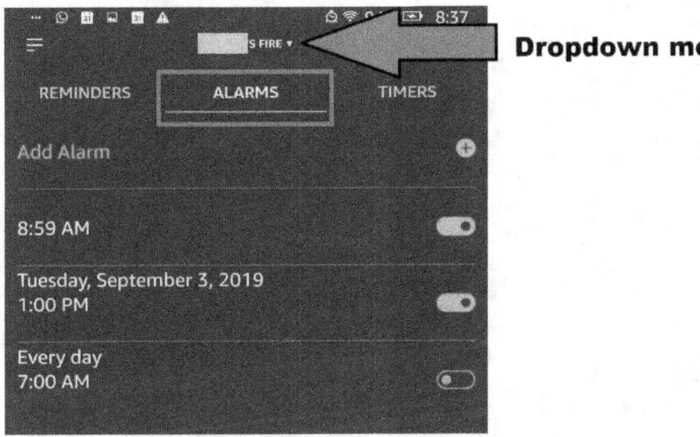

4. Select the **Alarms** tab.

5. Choose the alarm you want to delete, and then select **Delete alarm**.

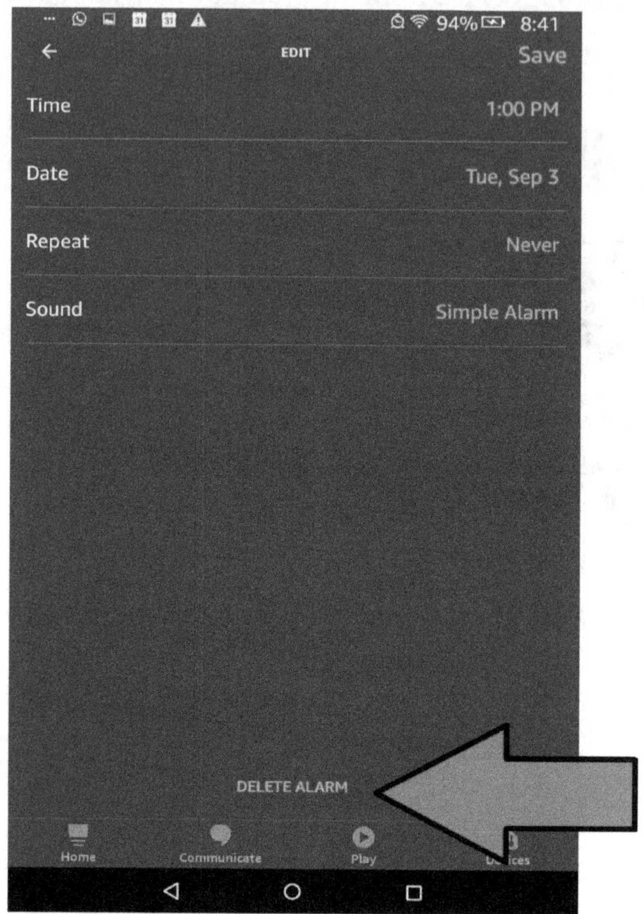

Tip: You may cancel an alarm with your voice. This will stop the alarm but may not delete it. For example, if you have any alarm set for 8 p.m. on Friday, say **Alexa cancel my alarm for 8 p.m. on Friday.** This will cancel this particular alarm.

To change your alarm sound:

1. Repeat steps 1 to 4 above.
2. Tap the alarm you want to manage.
3. Tap **Sound**.

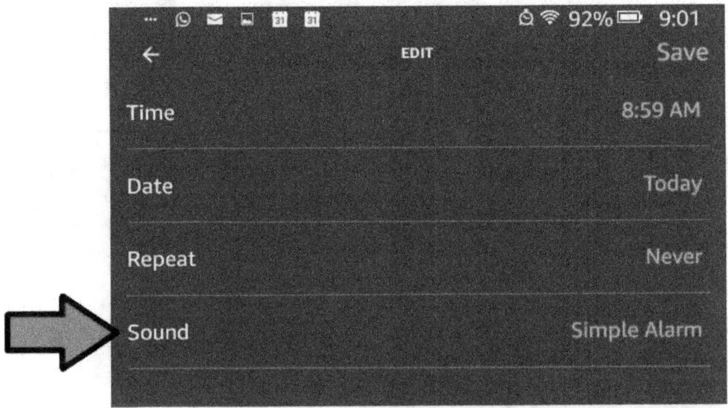

4. Scroll down and choose a sound. When you select a sound, a checkmark icon would appear next to it.

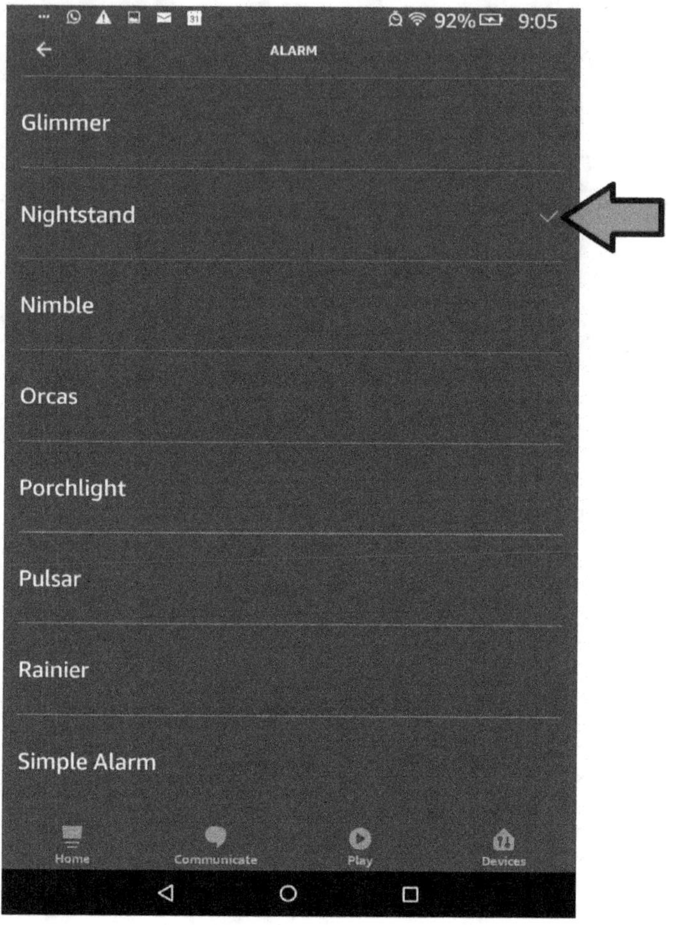

5. Tap the back arrow icon ![back arrow] found at the top of the screen.

6. Tap **Save** (found at the top of the screen) to save the changes.

Using Alexa with Timer

You can set a timer using this personal assistant. To do this, tap and hold the Home button until you see a blue line or say **Alexa**. Then try these example commands:

- **Set a timer for 30 minutes.**

- **Remove a minute from my timer.**

To stop the timer when it is sounding, say **Alexa, stop the timer**.

To know the status of your timer, tap and hold the Home button until you see a blue line or say Alexa, then say things like:

- **How much time is left on my timer?**

Tip: To dismiss a timer when it is sounding, tap the back button located at the bottom of the screen.

To edit/delete a timer:

1. Open the Alexa app and tap on the menu icon located at the top left corner of the screen.
2. Tap on **Reminders & Alarms**.
3. Tap on the **Timers** tab (found at the top of the screen).
4. Choose your device from the drop-down menu (if not currently displayed).

5. Tap on the timer you want to manage.
6. Select **Pause** to pause the timer or select **Delete Timer** to delete the timer.

You can also use your voice to delete an upcoming timer, simply say **Alexa cancel the timer for (amount of time).**

Using Alexa with Clock

You can ask Alexa what your local time is. In addition, it can also tell you the time in a specific place. To do this, tap and hold the Home button until you see a blue line or say **Alexa**, then try these example commands:

- **What is the time?**
- **What is the time in the New York?**

Using Alexa to Get Flight Information

You can also use this personal assistant to get information about a flight. This is a smarter way to know when a particular airplane will take off. To do this, tap and hold the Home button until you see a blue line or say Alexa, then try these example commands:

Alexa what is the flight status of Delta 400?

Alexa what is the flight time between New York City and Florida.

Listen to Your Audiobooks

Alexa can read audiobooks to you.

To read an audiobook you own, tap and hold the Home button until you see a blue line or hear a sound, then try these example commands:

- **Read (title)**
- **Play the book, (title)**
- **Read the audiobook, (title)**

To pause an audiobook, simply say **Alexa pause.** To resume, say **Alexa resume my audiobook**. You can also say **Alexa, continue**.

Please note that while listening to an audiobook, player controls will appear on the screen of your tablet in the form of a card. These keys can be used to control the audiobook. In addition, you can dismiss this card by pressing the back button ◁. You should see the player controls again by swiping down from the top of the screen.

To go back or forward in the audiobook by 30 seconds, say **Alexa, go back/forward**

To go to the next or previous chapter in an audiobook, say **Alexa, next chapter** or **previous chapter**.

Say **Alexa, go to chapter 4** to go to a specific chapter.

To stop reading in a future time, tap and hold the Home button and say **Stop reading the book in (amount of time) minutes/hours.**

Read Kindle Books with Alexa

Alexa can read eligible Kindle books using text-to-speech technology.

To read a Kindle book you own, tap and hold the Home button until you see a blue line or say Alexa, then try these example commands:

- **Read my Kindle book (title)**
- **Play the book (title)**
- **Read my book (title)**

To pause a Kindle book, say **Alexa, pause.** To resume, say **Alexa, resume my Kindle book.**

To move forward or backward in a Kindle book, say **Alexa, go back/forward.**

Please note that while listening to a Kindle book, player controls will appear on the screen of your tablet in the form of a card. These keys can be used to control the Kindle book. In addition, you can dismiss this card by tapping the back button. You should see the player controls again by swiping down from the top of the screen.

Buying Items Using Your Voice

If you are a Prime member, you can tell Alexa to order an item for you. To do this, you will first need to:

1. Open the Alexa app and tap on the menu icon located at the top left corner of the screen.

2. Tap on **Settings**.

3. Tap on **Alexa Account**.

4. Tap **Voice Purchasing**.

5. Tap an option:

   a. **Purchase by Voice**: Use the option to enable or disable voice purchasing. You may also need to enable your 1-Click payment method and billing address if you have not done so before.

   b. **Voice Code:** This option allows you to enter a 4-digit code that Alexa will ask for before you complete a purchase.

Aftcr this sctup, you may shop for Prime-Eligible items from Amazon using your voice. To order a product, tap and hold the Home button until you see a blue line or say Alexa, and then say things like:

Order me (item name)

To reorder an item, tap and hold the Home button and say **Reorder (item name)**

Please note that when ordering an item, Alexa may ask you some questions, just respond accordingly to confirm/decline.

To cancel an order immediately after placing it, say **Alexa, cancel my order.**

To add an item to your cart on Amazon, tap and hold the Home button and say **Add (item name) to my cart**.

To track your orders, say, **Alexa, Track my order** or say, **where is my stuff?**

Tip: To better manage your orders or contact a seller, go to amazon.com using a web browser.

In addition, you can set up recognized voices so that you can shop more confidently using Alexa. Simply perform the following operations:

1. Open the Alexa app and tap on the menu icon located at the top left corner of the screen.
2. Tap on **Settings**.
3. Tap on **Alexa Account**.
4. Tap **Recognized Voices**.
5. Select **Your Voice** and carefully follow the prompts.

Using Alexa to Get Traffic Information

You can use Alexa to get information about traffic situation on your route. To get this information, you will first need to tell Alexa what your route is. To do this:

1. Open the Alexa app and tap on the menu icon located at the top left corner of the screen.
2. Tap on **Settings**.
3. Select **Traffic**.
4. Enter your starting point and destination in the **From** and **To** sections and select **Save**.

After this setup, you can get traffic information about your route by asking Alexa a traffic question. To do this, say, Alexa, then try things like:

- **What's my commute?**
- **What's traffic like right now?**
- **How is my traffic?**

What about Math?

Alexa can also help you with some mathematics and conversion. For example, you can tell Alexa "**What is the square root of four?**" You may also say "**How many centimeters are in one foot?**" or "**What is 60 factorial**?" and so on.

In addition, note that you can say all the examples given above in other ways; the most important thing is to get Alexa to understand what you are saying.

Using Alexa to Get Definitions

You can quickly check for the meaning of a word by asking Alexa. For example, you may say "**Alexa, What is the meaning of flabbergasted?**"

Using Alexa with Wikipedia

You can use Alexa to get information from Wikipedia.

To get Wikipedia information, say, **Alexa, Wikipedia [subject].**

Using Alexa To Get General Information

If you will like to know more about a thing you can ask Alexa. For example, you may say **Alexa, What is the shape of the earth?**

Funny Sides of Alexa

One of the main features that make Alexa interesting is its ability to give a reply in funny manner. This all depends on what you ask it. Some of the questions you can ask it to get funny replies are given below:

- **Do you sleep?**

- **Do you eat?**

- **Do you like your job?**

- **Do you have a brain?**

- **Are you lying?**

The list of questions you can ask Alexa to get funny replies goes on like that. As I have said before, it all depends on the type of question you ask this assistant.

Using Alexa Show Mode

When Show Mode is activated, you can use the Alexa on your tablet like you use the Echo Show. When Show Mode is enabled, Fire tablet will show Alexa screen and will display the responses to your question on this screen. You may not be able to use apps while the Show Mode is enabled. Also, the Show Mode makes your tablet to go into landscape mode.

Please note that Show Mode might only work after you have connected your tablet to a power source.

To use the Show Mode:

1. Connect your tablet to a power source.
2. Swipe down from the top of the screen, and tap the status switch next to **Show Mode**.

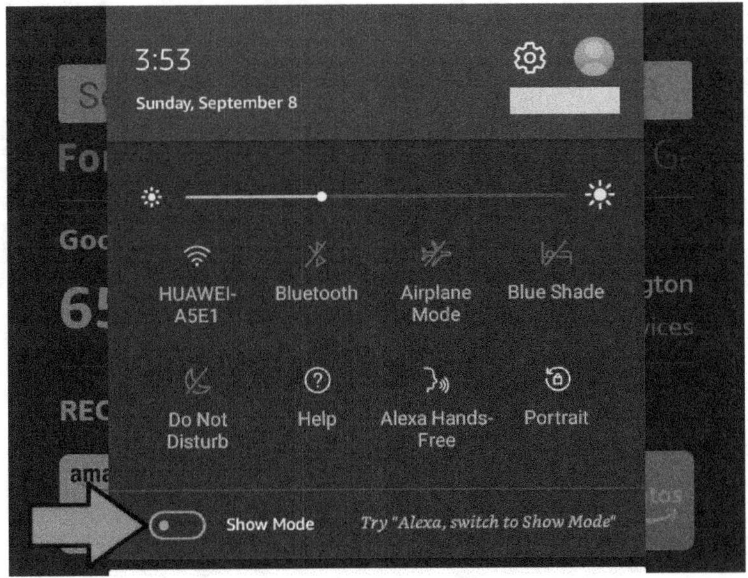

3. Ask Alexa a question of your choice.

4. To exit the Show mode, repeat step 2 above.

Calling and Messaging on Fire Tablet

You can call and message supported devices using your Fire tablet.
To get started, you may need to sign up for Alexa's calling.

Signing up for Alexa Calling

1. Open the Alexa app.

2. Tap the conversation icon located at the bottom of the
   screen.

3. Follow the on-screen instructions to complete the signing up
   process.

Using the Alexa Drop In

Drop In feature allows you to drop in on your contacts and
connected Alexa devices. Drop In is different from voice call in that
you get automatically connected to contact (or Alexa devices) you
drop in on. This means the contact doesn't need to manually answer
your call. When you use the Drop In feature, you should begin to
immediately hear anything near the microphone of the device you
are dropping in on.

To drop in on a contact, you have to manually add the contact. In
addition, the contact has to allow your Drop In request.

Furthermore, if you use an Alexa device with a screen (such as your Fire tablet) to drop in on another Alexa device with screen, you should be automatically connected to a video chat. To switch off the video option, simply say **Alexa Video Off**.

Using and managing Drop In feature

Please note that you may need to sign up for Alexa calling before using the **Drop In** feature. Please see **Signing up for Alexa Calling** to know how to sign up for Alexa Calling.

To use and manage the Drop In feature:

1. Open the Alexa app and tap the conversation icon . Alternatively, tap on **Set Up Drop In** and follow the prompts.

2. To allow a contact to drop in, click on the contact icon (located at the top of the screen) and select a contact. Then select status switch next to **Contact can Drop In Anytime**.

3. To revoke a Drop In permission for a contact, click on the contact icon. Then select the status switch next to **Contact can Drop In Anytime**.

4. To edit your Alexa contacts, simply do so using the local contact app on your tablet. Alexa should automatically sync with the changes made. Contacts from your Address book who also use Alexa Calling & Messaging should automatically appear in the contacts list in your Alexa app.

5. To use your Fire tablet to drop in, say, Alexa, Drop in on [device's name]. To end the Drop In, say **Alexa, hang up**.

Please note that you can't drop in on Alexa app, but you can use Alexa app to drop in on other Alexa devices.

6. To use the Alexa app to drop in, tap the Drop In icon and select the name of the device you want to drop in on. Alternatively, select a contact and tap the Drop In icon. To end the Drop In, tap the screen and select the Hang Up (red) button.

Using Alexa to Make Calls

You can use Alexa to call mobile and landline numbers and other supported Alexa devices.

Please note that you may need to sign up for Alexa Calling before you can make calls. Please see page 62 to know how to sign up for Alexa Calling.

To make, end and manage a call:

1. To call a supported Alexa device, say, **Alexa, call [name of the Alexa device]**.

2. To call a mobile/landline number you don't have its details in your contact app, say, **Alexa, call [mobile/landline number]**. If you have the contact, say **Alexa call [contact's name]**.

   You could also say, **Alexa, call [contact's name] on his home phone**.

3. To answer a call, say **Answer**. To ignore a call, say **Ignore**.

4. To reduce or increase the volume, say, **Alexa, turn the volume up/down**.

5. To end a call, say, **Alexa, hang up**.

Note: Alexa Calling does not support calls to all types of numbers. For example, you may not be able to call some international numbers using Alexa calling.

Sending and Receiving Messages on Alexa

You can send a message to others supported Alexa devices using your voice or Alexa app. To do this:

1. Say, **Alexa, send a message to [device name or contact's name]**. Alexa would then prompt you for the message. Follow the voice prompts to complete the process.

2. To use the Alexa app to send a message, open the Alexa app and tap the conversation icon found at the bottom of the screen. Tap the message icon located at the top of the screen and select a contact from the contact list. Then type your message.

Alexa's Settings

The settings tab under the Alexa app allows you to manage Alexa's functions. To access Alexa settings:

1. Open the Alexa app [image] and tap on the menu icon [image] located at the top left corner of the screen.

2. Tap on **Settings**

3. Tap an option.

Tip: Settings allow you to customize your Alexa in a special way. Whenever you think of giving Alexa a special tweak, go to settings.

Troubleshooting Alexa

Although much effort has been put into making this virtual assistant, it is possible that Alexa will misbehave at one time or the other. When this happens, there are few things to do.

- **Ensure that you are connected to a strong network**: If you have bad or no internet connection, Alexa may not work properly. Therefore the first thing to check when Alexa starts to misbehave is the internet connection.

- **Speak clearly in a silent place**: Make sure you are speaking clearly and try to avoid background noise. In addition, try to be specific in your commands.

- **Try to Restart Your Tablet**: If you find out that all that we have mentioned above does not work, you may try restarting your device because it may be that it is your device that is confused and not Alexa.

The Word Runner

This feature allows you to fix your gaze on the tablet while the words you are reading move by themselves. It saves you the effort of moving your look to different parts of the screen in order to read a book. This feature is also made in such a way that it automatically slows down when comes across a difficult word or punctuation. You have the option to choose a speed with which this feature move words when you are reading a book. If you miss something while reading, tap the screen to pause the Word Runner. When you are done, just tap the screen again. To learn more about word runner, please go to reading books with the new Fire tablets (see page 135).

Using the Web and the Apps

Silk Browser

Fire tablet is preloaded with Silk browser to cater to your browsing needs. Please note that the information provided here may vary if Amazon makes any update to Silk browser.

Browsing web pages

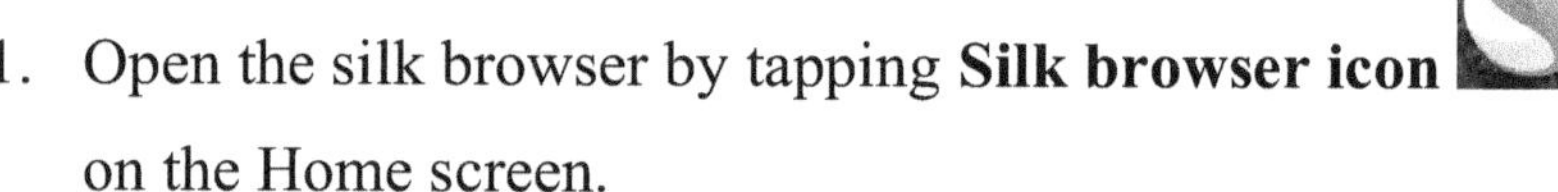

1. Open the silk browser by tapping **Silk browser icon** on the Home screen.

2. Type the web address into the URL input field, and tap search/go button (the arrow button on the virtual keyboard). As you type into the address bar, Silk browser will make search suggestions based on your default search engine, to launch any of the suggested webpage or search term, tap on it.

3. To go back to the previous webpage, tap the menu icon (the three dots icon, see the screenshot below) and tap on the back arrow. To go forward, tap the forward icon.

4. You can navigate web pages and get more done with the following keys which are explained below.

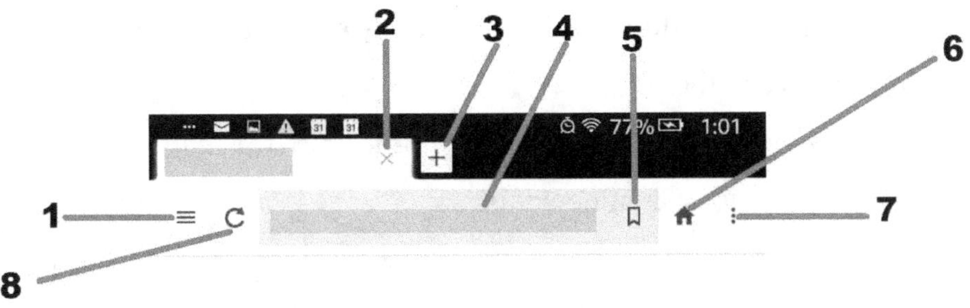

Number	Function
1.	Left Panel icon: Use this to access features like settings, bookmarks, history, etc.
2.	Close a webpage
3.	Add tab: Use this to add another browsing tab
4.	URL input/search field
5	Bookmark icon: Use this to add a webpage to your bookmark list
6	Home icon: Use this to go to the home page.
7	Menu icon: Use this to access features like **Forward & Backward buttons**, **Private browsing, Add bookmark, Share, Print, Request desktop site** and **Find in Page.**
8	Reload icon

Note: The **onscreen icons** may disappear when scrolling down a webpage.

Opening multiple pages/tabs

You can open multiple pages on Silk browser and switch back and forth between them.

1. Open the browser by tapping on **Silk browser icon**

2. Select '+' to open a new tab.

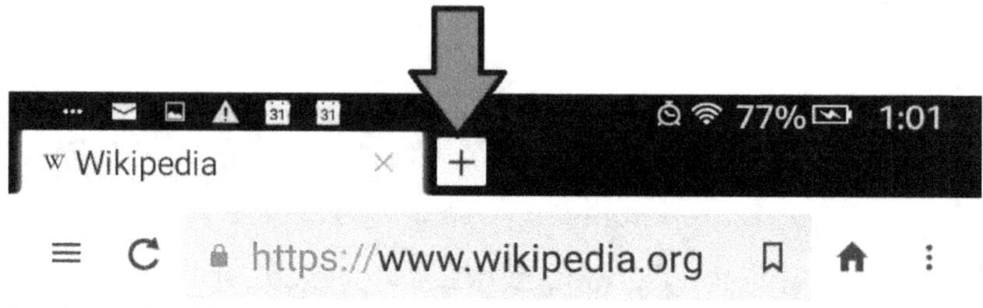

3. Type a web address into the URL field of the new tab and tap the search/go button (the arrow button on the virtual keyboard).

4. To switch back and forth between currently opened tabs, tap the small window directly on top of the webpage you want to switch to.

5. To close a tab, select the **X** icon.

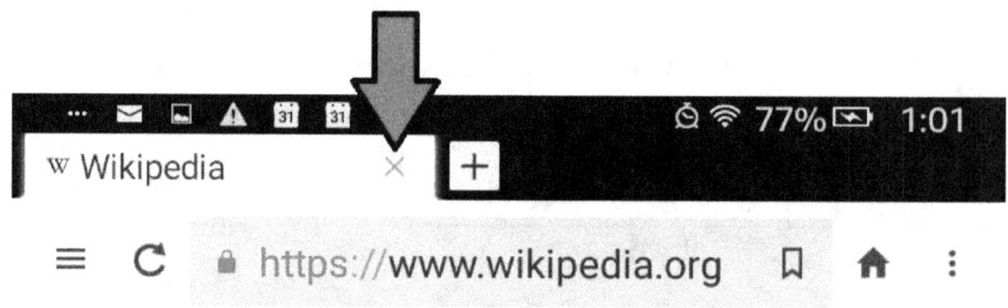

Hint:

- To zoom in, place two fingers on the screen and spread them apart. To zoom out, move your two fingers closer together.

Please note that not all webpages support zooming, but you can force a page to zoom (see page 81).

Bookmarking your favorite webpages

You can manually add a bookmark if you know the web address of a web page.

> **To add a bookmark**

1. Tap on the **Silk browser icon** on the Home screen.

2. Enter the web address of the page you want to bookmark into the URL page and launch it.

3. Tap the bookmark icon (on the address bar).

4. To view your bookmarks, swipe in from the left edge of the screen to open the left panel. Then tap on **Bookmarks**.

5. To edit a bookmark, swipe in from the left edge of the screen to open the left panel and then tap on **Bookmarks.** Then tap the menu icon next to the bookmark you want to edit and select **Edit**. Enter necessary information and select **Save**.

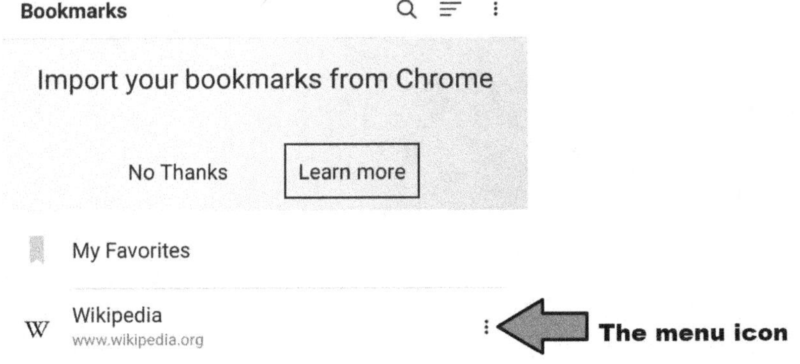

6. To remove a bookmark, swipe in from the left edge of the screen to open the left panel and tap on **Bookmarks.** Then tap the menu icon next to the bookmark you want to remove and select **Remove.** Select **Remove** again when prompted.

Accessing History

1. Open Silk web browser 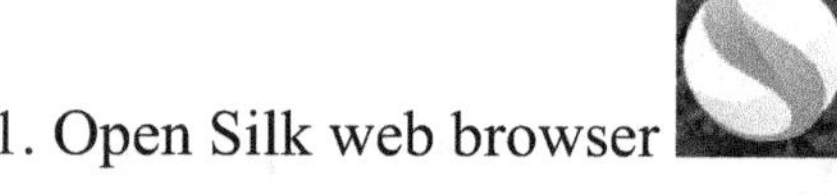.

2. Swipe from the left edge of the screen and tap on **History.**

3. Tap the **X** icon to delete individual webpages on the history page.

4. To delete all the browsing history, tap the delete icon , select all that you want to clear using the dialogue that appears and then tap **Clear data.**

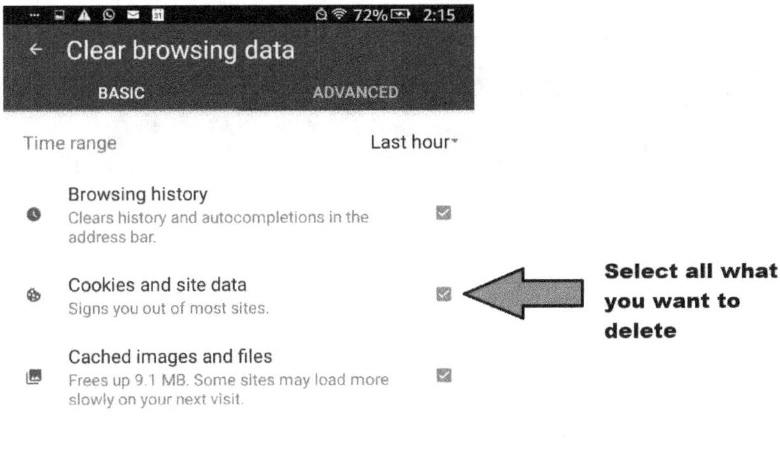

5. To access more history options (such as password), select **Advanced** and then select all the items you want to delete. Select **Clear Data**.

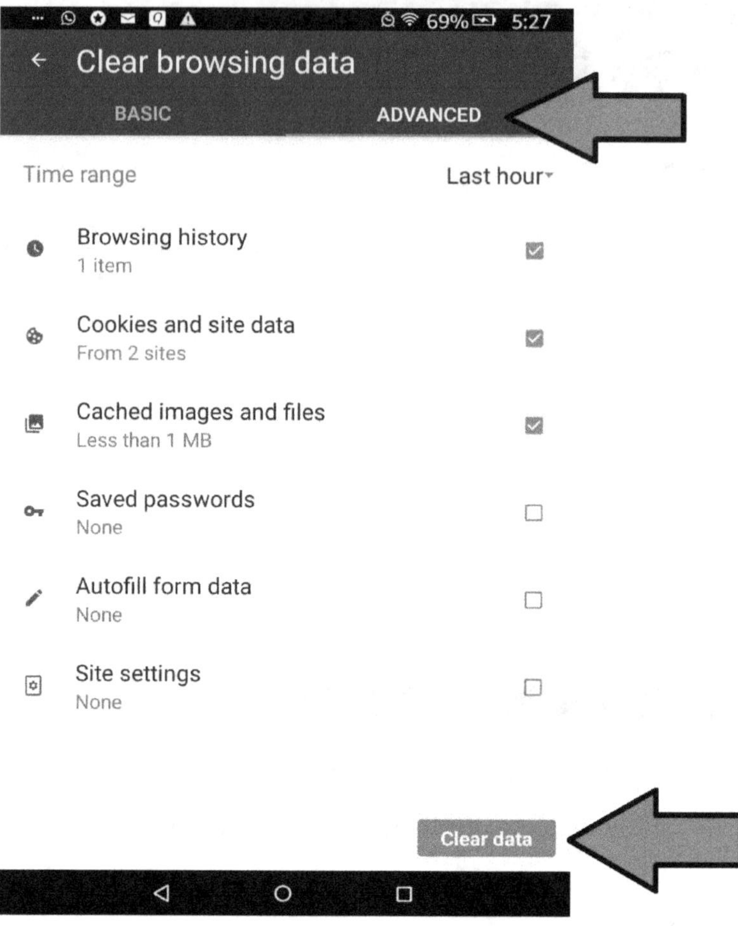

Loading the Desktop View of a Webpage

1. Tap on the **Silk browser icon** on Home screen.

2. Enter a web address into the URL address bar and launch it.

3. Tap on the **Menu** icon.

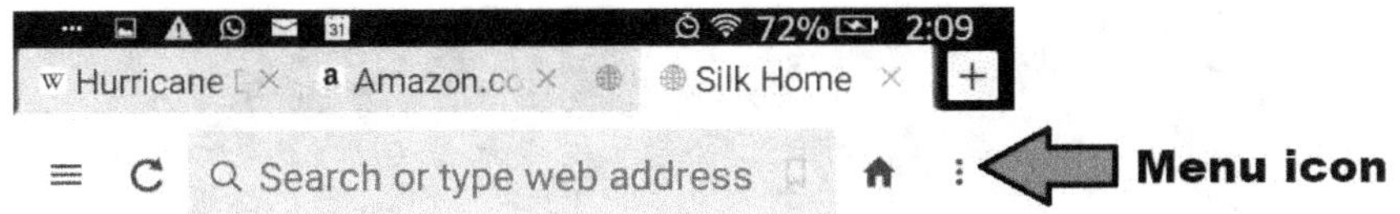

4. Tap on **Desktop Site**. To go back to the mobile site, select **Mobile Site.**

Hint: You may be unable to properly view some sites with flash contents in desktop mode, requesting mobile sites of websites like these may solve this problem.

Getting Extra Options on Silk Browser

There are still some options that are not present on the menu tab or the left panel. To access these options, open a webpage and tap and hold on a link, image file or video file on the webpage. Some of the options that may be available include **copy link text, download image, open in a new tab, download link** among others. Please note that the options you see are contextual. For example, the options you see when you tap and hold a link is different from what you see when you tap and hold an image.

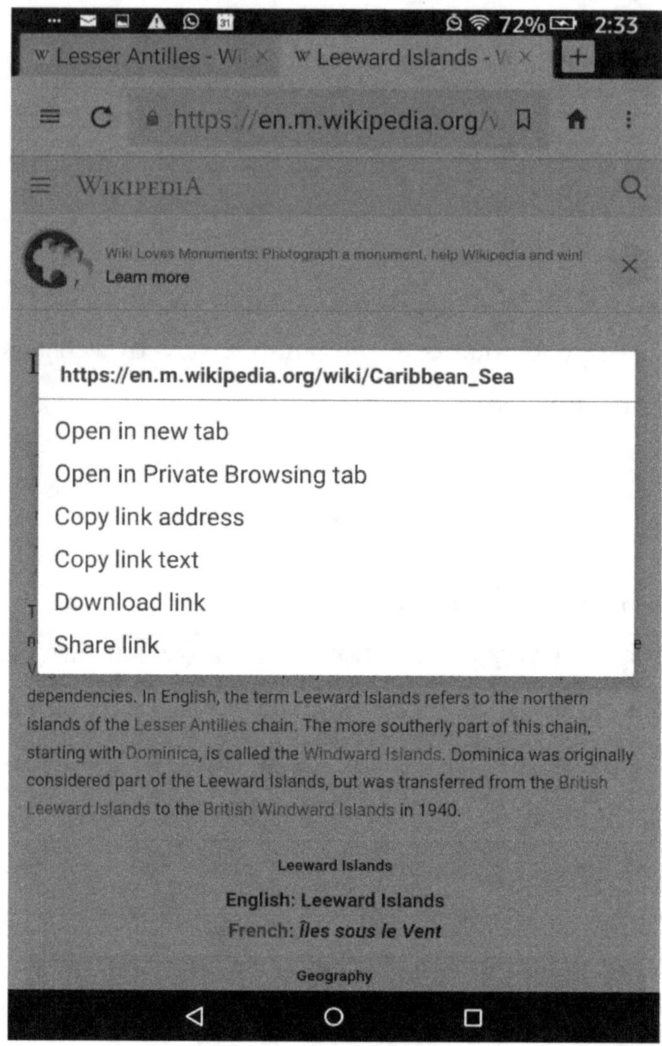

Downloading Files and Using the Download Folder

The download folder contains your downloaded files and these may include documents file, video files, image files, and webpages.

To access the download file, swipe from the left edge of the screen and tap on **Downloads.**

To download a file, click on the file and wait for the download to complete.

To download a link, image or video, tap and hold on the link/image/video and select the corresponding option.

Notes: The downloaded documents such as PDFs will be saved under **DOCS**, while downloaded images and videos will be saved under **Amazon Photos**.

While trying to download a file, you may be prompted that the file might harm your device, tap **OK** to continue the downloading process if you are sure of the security of the file.

If a file is downloading, it should show up in the notification bar, to access the notification bar, swipe down from the top of the screen.

Printing a Webpage and Saving It as PDF

To print a webpage or save a webpage as PDF:

1. Tap the menu icon ⋮ (the three dots icon located at the top right corner of the screen) and select **Print.** A dialog box will then appear for you to select a printer.

2. If you want to save the webpage as a PDF, select **Save as PDF** from the drop-down menu.

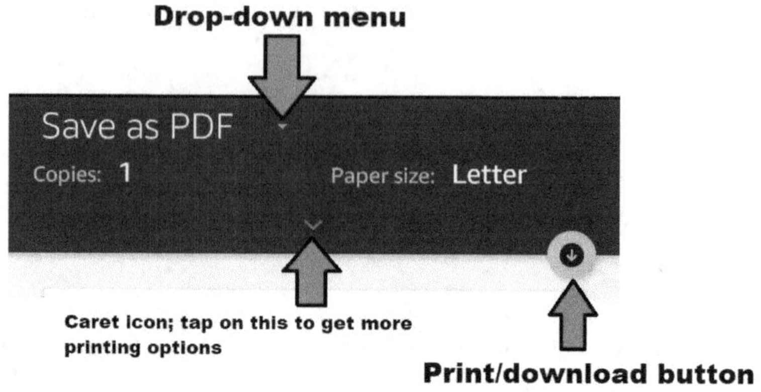

3. Tap the download icon 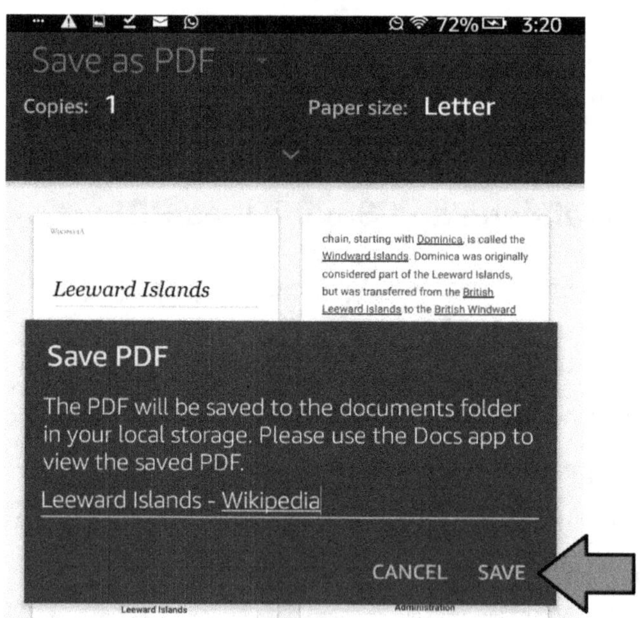 and enter a memorable name. Tap **Save** to save the PDF.

Go to **Docs** app 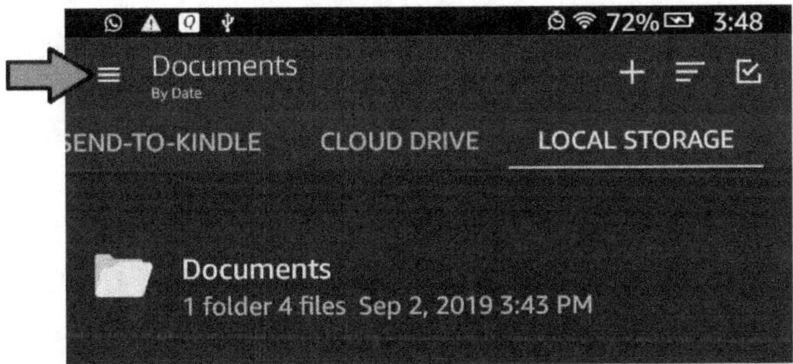 on the Home screen to locate the PDF you
just downloaded. If you can't see the downloaded file, click on the
menu icon ☰ located at the top left part of the screen and select
Documents.

4. If you want to print a webpage, Fire tablet should be able to
   find your wireless printer and give you the option to add it.
   After adding your printer, use the caret icon to customize
   your printing. (Please make sure your device's Wi-Fi is On
   when connecting a wireless printer).
5. You will have the option to select those pages you want to
   print from the print preview that appears. To include/exclude
   a page, tap the thumbnail corresponding to the page. When a
   page is deselected, the page thumbnail appears grey.

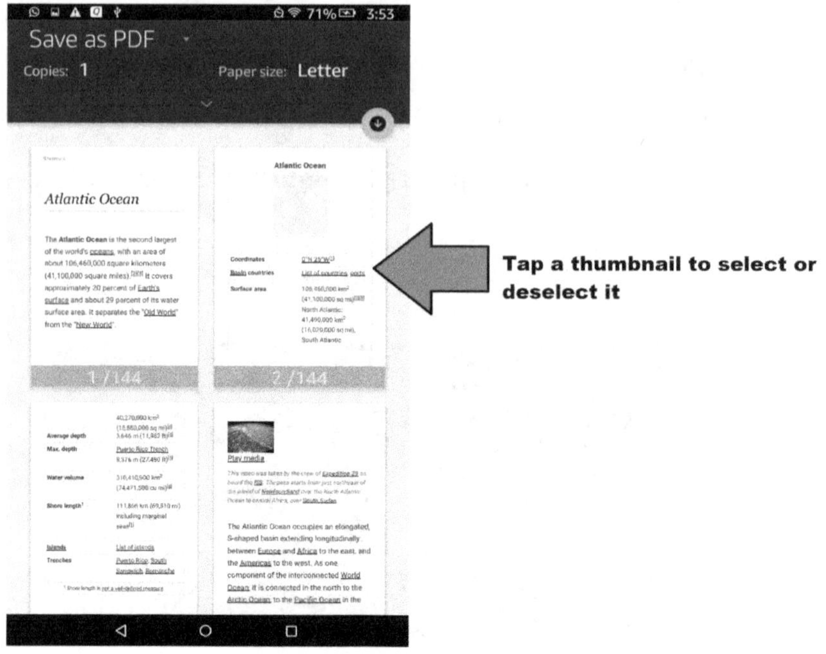

6. When you are done, click on the download icon .

Changing the Search Engine

The default search engine on your Silk browser might not be what you like. To change the search engine to the one you prefer, please follow the steps below:

1. While the Silk browser is opened, swipe in from the left edge of the screen and select **Settings**.

2. Select **Advanced**.

3. Tap on **Search engine** and select a search engine.

Managing the Settings under Silk Browser

1. Open the Silk Browser from the app grid.

2. Swipe in from the left edge of the screen and tap on **Settings** to view the following options:

   a. **Payment methods**: Tap this to add your payment information to the Silk browser.

   b. **Passwords**: Tap this to access saved passwords.

   c. **Addresses and more**: Use this to add home/office addresses to the Silk browser.

   d. **Accessibility:** This include:

      i. **Text Scaling:** Use the slider to increase the size of the text in the box. To zoom a webpage, simply double-tap on a paragraph when viewing the webpage.

      ii. **Force Enable Zoom**: When this option is selected, it overrides a website's request to prevent zooming.

      iii. **Reading View**: When this is enabled, the Silk browser offers to show articles in Reading View, when supported.

   e. **Silk Home**: Use this tab to manage what appears on the Silk Homepage.

   f. **Privacy**: Use this to manage Silk browser Privacy settings. Privacy settings include:

      i. **Safe Browsing**: When this is enabled, the Silk browser attempts to protect you and your device from dangerous sites. Please note that when this is enabled, you may need to send URLs of some pages you visit to Amazon when your security is at risk.

   ii. **Do Not Track** – Use this setting to tell websites not to display ads based on your browsing or search history. However, please note that websites may choose to ignore these requests.

  iii. **Clear Browsing Data**: Use this option to delete your browser history, which may include websites you've saved, saved passwords, and personal information added to forms.

g. **Advanced:** This gives you the option to change the **search engine**, access **site settings,** and access Silk browser information. **Site Settings** include:

   i. **Cookies:** These are small information (packets) stored on your browser to improve your browsing experience when using a site.

  ii. **Location**: Use this option to allow sites to request access to your location. When a website wants to use your location data, the Silk browser may prompt you. Tap **Allow** to send your location data to the website, or tap **Decline** to ignore the request.

iii. **Camera**: Use this option to allow sites to request the use of the camera on your device.

iv. **Microphone:** Use this option to enable websites to make a request to use the microphone on your device.

v. **JavaScript:** Websites use JavaScript to improve the browsing experience. Please note that many sites may not function properly if this option is disabled.

vi. **Pop-ups and redirects:** Use this option to prevent pop-ups and redirects. Pop-ups are small windows that suddenly appear when you are browsing. Some pop-ups are actually wanted but some are just intruders.

Hint: If Silk browser starts misbehaving, try to clear the browsing data. To learn how to clear browsing data, go to history on page 72.

Using other Fire tablet apps

You can access any preinstalled app on your tablet by tapping its icon. You may be required to accept terms of service when using an app for the first time. To access more features on a particular app, swipe from the left edge of the screen to bring out the left panel.

Communication

Using The Email App

You may add more than one email account to your email app. Note that your email is automatically synced with Calendar and Contacts app on your tablet (unless this function is not supported by your email provider). The Email app supports Gmail, Yahoomail, Outlook, etc.

To set up an email account:

1. From the Home screen, tap on the **Email** app icon.
2. If you are using the Email app for the first time, enter your email address, and follow the onscreen instructions to connect your email account.
3. If you have added one account and wish to add another email account, while in the Email app, swipe from the left edge of the screen and tap **Add Account**, and follow the onscreen instructions.
4. You can repeat the steps above to add another email account.

Note: If your email is not recognized, you will see the option to manually add your account using the advanced setup screen. To manually add your account, you will need to obtain your email account information from your email provider.

We will advise that you contact your email provider or system administrator in order to set up your email on Fire tablet.

Managing your email account

1. Tap on the **Email** app icon 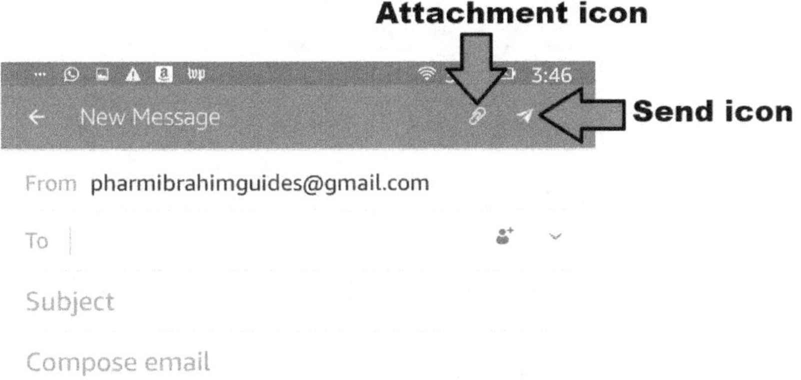 from the app grid.

2. To compose an email, tap the pen icon (found at the bottom of the screen) and then fill the address, subject and message sections. To add an attachment tap on the **attachment** icon (the clip icon). When done tap on **Send** icon.

3. To save an email as a draft, tap on the menu icon, and select **Save Draft**. To discard a message, select the menu icon and select **Discard Draft**.

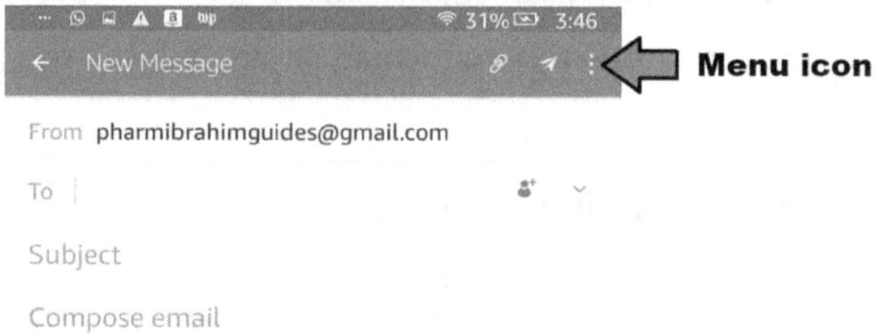

4. To read email, tap on the email you want to read.

5. To reply a message, tap on the message and then tap on the

    Reply icon 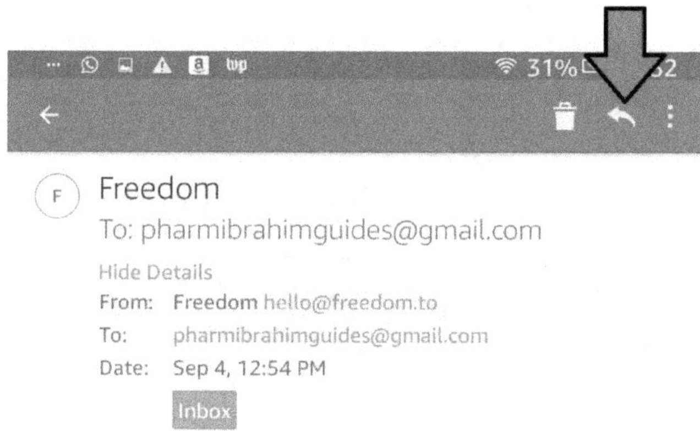 (the arrow-like icon).

6. To delete an email, while viewing an email tap **Delete** icon
    (found at the top of the screen).

7. Use the search icon (magnifying lens icon) to search for
    specific emails in your inbox.

Downloading Attachment

Check for the **paperclip** icon to know whether an email is having an attachment or not.

1. Tap on Email app from the app grid screen.
2. Tap on the message with an attachment and scroll down (if needed) to see the attachment.
3. Tap on the attachment and allow it to download.
4. To save an attachment, tap on **Save** next to the thumbnail of the attachment.
5. After the completion of the download, tap the attachment again to view the attachment.

Note: After saving an attachment, if the attachment is a photo or video, check your **Amazon Photos** app to access it. If the attachment is a document, check the **Docs** app to access it.

Managing the Email Settings

Use these settings to customize your experience when using the

Email app. To access settings, open the Email app 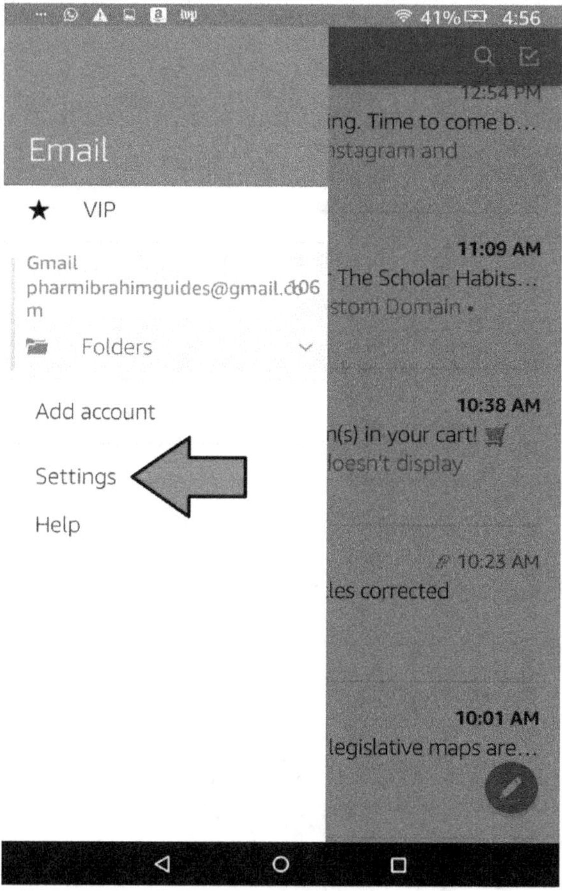 and swipe

in from the left edge of the screen. Then select **Settings**.

Generally, there are four primary tabs under Email app settings and
they are:

- **Email Settings**: This option allows you to manage settings like replies, attachments, email images, conversation settings, among others.

- **Contact settings**: This option allows you to manage contact settings.

- **Calendar settings**: This option allows you to manage calendar settings.

- **Accounts**: Tap on any account under this tab to manage settings like signature, default account, account name, account deletion, among others.

Hint: Usually, you can get more information about a particular setting by reading the text under it.

Using Facebook, Goodreads, and Twitter

You can link your device to Facebook, Goodreads or Twitter account.

To link a social account:

1. From **Settings,** tap **My Accounts,** and then tap **Social Networks.**

2. Then tap on **Connect** next to the social network you want to connect with. Follow the prompts to complete the linking process.

3. Note that you can unlink your social account at any time.

Personal Information

Contacts

This app allows you to create and manage a list of your personal or business contacts. You can save names, mobile phone numbers, home phone numbers, email addresses, and more.

To create a contact:

1. Tap on the contact app.

2. Tap on the new contact icon located at the lower right corner of the screen.

3. Carefully fill in the details and save the contact.

To manage a contact

1. Open the app grid and tap on **Contacts**.

2. Tap on a contact from the list.

3. Use the onscreen icons to perform different tasks of your choice.

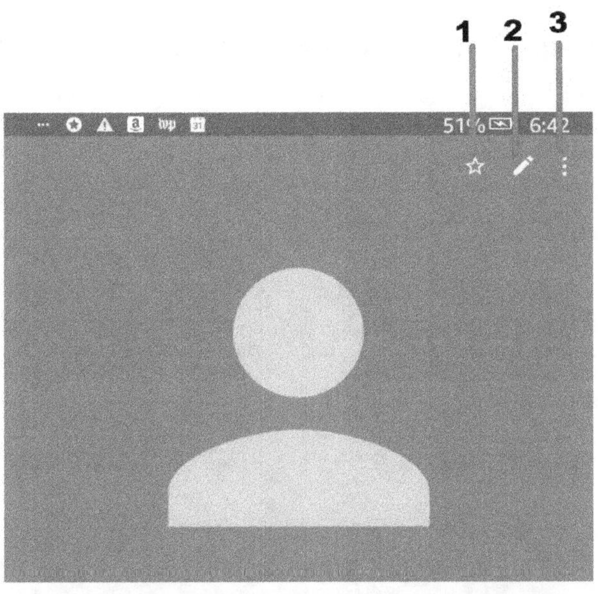

Number	Function
1.	Favorite icon: tap this to add a contact to your Favorites/VIP list. To access the Favorite list, open the Contacts app and tap **Favorites** tab (found at the top of the screen).
2.	Tap this **pen icon** to change contact details.
3.	Tap **menu icon** to delete a contact or share a contact

Hint: From Contacts app, tap the menu icon (found at the top of the screen) to get more options.

In addition, you can search the Contact app by tapping on the search

button (the magnifying lens icon) located at the top of the

screen.

Accessibility Features – The Special Features for Easy Usage

Accessibility services are special features for those with physical challenges. It also provides you the opportunity to control your tablet in a special way.

VoiceView Demystified

VoiceView allows you to hear what is happening on the screen as you touch/interact with your screen.

To turn on the VoiceView

1. Swipe down from the top of the screen to access the Quick Actions panel, and then tap **Settings** .
2. Scroll down and tap on **Accessibility**.
3. Tap on **VoiceView Screen Reader**.
4. Switch on the slider next to **VoiceView.**
5. Carefully read instructions that appear and follow the voice prompts.

To turn off the VoiceView

Triple-press the power button to turn off the VoiceView.

Customizing the VoiceView

Note: Because the VoiceView is on, the first tap will select an item and you will then need to double-tap the screen to access the selected item or perform a specific action on the item.

To customize the VoiceView when this feature is On:

1. While on the Home screen, swipe up with three fingers to access more app icons and then tap on **Settings**. Alternatively, while on the Home screen, swipe right until you hear Settings being read to you.

2. Then double-tap on the screen to open the settings menu.

3. Scroll down with three fingers and tap on **Accessibility**. Then double-tap the screen to activate. Alternatively, swipe right until you hear Accessibility being read to you, then double-tap the screen to open the Accessibility menu.

4. Tap **VoiceView Screen Reader** to select it, and then double-tap the screen to open its options. The following options are available:

    *   **VoiceView**: Tap this to activate or deactivate VoiceView.

    *   **VoiceView Shortcut**: When this option is enabled, you can triple-press the power button to turn on/off the VoiceView.

    *   **Typing Style**: Use this option to select how you type texts when VoiceView is on.

    *   **Speech**: Use this tab to access settings like reading speed, speech volume, etc.

    *   **Braille**: Use this tab to access braille settings.

- **VoiceView Tutorial**: Use this option to access tutorials on VoiceView.

Using the VoiceView

VoiceView allows you to navigate your tablet with some specific gestures.

Note: To turn on the **VoiceView at any point in time (without going to the settings)**, triple-press the power button. Alternatively, long press the power button until you hear an alert from your tablet, and then place two fingers (slightly apart) on the screen and hold it for five-ten seconds. It is recommended you avoid placing the two fingers on any icons.

The following actions can be done when **VoiceView** is turned **on.**

1. **To go to the Home screen:** Quickly swipe your finger up then left in one stroke.

2. **To go back to the previous screen/page:** Quickly swipe down and then left in one stroke with a finger.

3. **To open an item, icon or menu:** If you don't know (or cannot see) the location of the item, icon, or menu on the screen, swipe right or left using your finger until the name of that particular item you want to open is read to you and then double-tap on any part of the screen to open it. If you know (or can see) the location of item, icon, or menu on screen, tap the item/icon/menu and then double-tap on any part of the screen to open/access it.

4. **To explore/select menus/items/icons on the screen:** Drag your finger over that item (as if you want to gently clean the surface bearing that item with your finger) until the name of that item is read to you.

5. **To move from one icon/item/menu to another on the screen:** swipe right or left using your finger until the name of that particular item you want to open is read to you.

6. **To Open Quick Actions and Notifications Panel:** Swipe down from the top of the screen with **three fingers.**

7. **To open the left panel:** Swipe from the left edge of the screen with three fingers.

8. **Type on the keyboard:** Slowly move a finger over the keys so that your tablet reads the keys to you. When you hear the letter of your choice, lift up your finger to add the letter to what you are typing.

9. **To Unlock the screen:** Swipe up from the bottom of the screen with two fingers.

Reading with VoiceView

VoiceView allows you to read books with certain gestures.

To start reading:

From the book you want to read, swipe down from the top of the page with three fingers. Make sure that the reading toolbar is not opened while doing this.

To pause or stop reading:

Tap the screen with three fingers.

To change reading voice:

1. While on the Home screen, swipe down from the top of the screen with three fingers to open Quick Actions.
2. Then tap the **Settings** to select it.
3. Then double-tap on the screen to open the settings menu.
4. Tap on **Keyboard & Language** to select it and then double-tap to open the options under it.
5. Tap on **Text-to-Speech** and then double-tap the screen.
6. Tap on **Default Voice** and then double-tap the screen. Choose an option. To go back to the previous page, quickly swipe down and then left in one stroke with a finger.

Note: Text-to-Speech voice can read in your device language. However, not all languages are supported.

To turn a page

Using three fingers, swipe left with to go to the next page or swipe right to go to the previous page.

Screen Magnifier

This option allows you to use certain gestures to magnify your screen so that you may better see what is on the screen.

To turn on screen magnifier

1. Swipe down from the top of the screen to access the Quick

    Actions panel, and then tap **Settings** 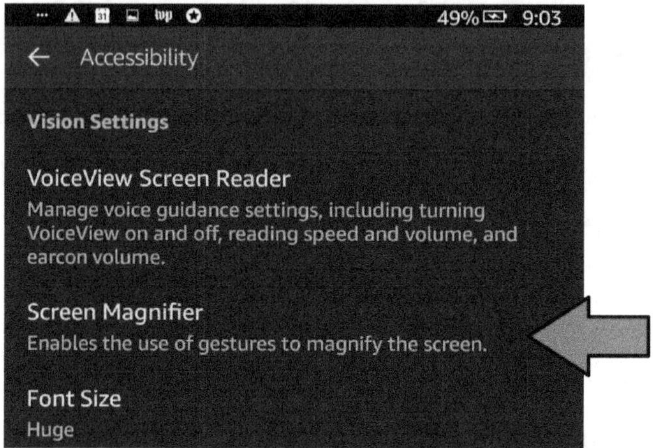.

2. Scroll down and tap on **Accessibility.**

3. Tap the switch next to **Screen Magnifier** and then tap **OK.**

When the Screen magnifier is on, you can perform any of these actions:

i. Zoom in: Triple tap on the screen with a finger. If you just want to temporarily magnify the screen, triple tap on the screen with a finger and hold, to see other parts of the screen, drag your finger across the screen.

ii. Pan: Place two fingers slightly apart on the screen and then drag it across the screen.

iii. To zoom in or out after activating Screen magnifier: Use your two fingers to pinch inward or outward until you get the magnification of your choice.

iv. Turn on Screen Magnifier during device setup: Go to **Settings** > **Accessibility** > **Screen Magnifier**.

Using the Braille with Fire Tablet

To connect braille to your Fire tablet:

1. Swipe down from the top of the screen to access the Quick Actions panel, and then tap **Settings**.

2. Scroll down and tap on **Accessibility**.

3. Tap on **VoiceView Screen Reader**.

4. Tap the status swicth next to **VoiceView** to enable it. Then tap on **Braille** and double tap the screen to open it. Please note that you would need to enable VoiceView to use Braille. Please go to the section above on page 93 to learn more about **VoiceView**.

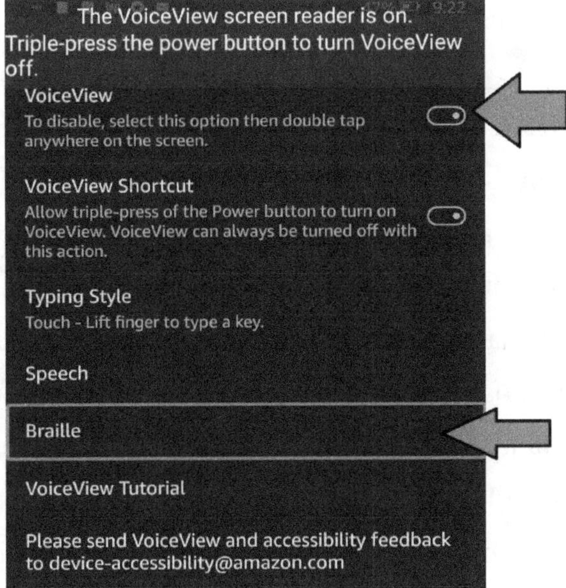

5. Tap on **Pair Bluetooth Braille Display**. Then double-tap to open.

6. Follow the voice prompts to finish the connection.

Managing the Hearing Settings

Hearing settings are features that enable you to customize sound settings.

To convert Stereo to mono:

1. Swipe down from the top of the screen to access the Quick Actions panel, and then tap **Settings** .

2. Scroll down and tap on **Accessibility.**

3. Under the **Hearing Settings**, Tap the switch next to **Convert Stereo to Mono** to disable the stereo sound.

Note: Disabling the stereo sound enables you to play all audio in a single channel, this may be important if you have a hearing aid in one ear or you are using a single ear bud.

Enabling Closed Captioning

Closed captioning is a feature that allows hearing impaired individuals to have a visual display (usually in form of text) of the audio portion of a program. It can be likened to subtitling.

For those videos that have close captioning enable, you should be able to view the closed captioning of those videos while watching it on Amazon Instant Video. Look out for **CC** icon when searching for videos on Amazon Instant Videos to know whether they support close captioning. You may also access the closed captioning feature on your Silk browser. To customize closed captioning to your taste, visit **www.amazon.com/cc**

1. Swipe down from the top of the screen to access the Quick Actions panel, and then tap **Settings**.

2. Scroll down and tap on **Accessibility.**

3. Under the **Hearing Settings**, tap the switch next to **Closed Captioning.**

To customize Closed Captions

1. Repeat the first three steps above

2. Tap **Closed Captioning Preferences** to customize your settings for:

   - **Text**: Use this to adjust text size, color, opacity, font, and edge style.

   - **Text Background**: Use this to select the color and opacity for the text's background.

   - **Window Background**: Use this to select the color and opacity for the Closed Captioning window.

   - If you want to use the settings you selected for Closed Captioning on Amazon Video captions, tap **On** next to **Use Amazon Web Settings for Amazon Video Captions**.

   - To reset to default settings, tap **Reset to Defaults**.

TOOLS

Amazon FreeTime Demystified

Amazon FreeTime allows you to create individual profiles for your children and customize a reading goal for them. As a parent, you have the opportunity to track the reading progress of your children. Kids earn achievements in the form of rewards that help them keep track of their personal reading accomplishments. When Amazon FreeTime is active, access to Kindle Store, the Silk Browser, Goodreads, in-app purchases and Social media features can either be blocked or restricted so that your kids only access what you want. In addition, children can only read books added to their library.

How set-up Amazon FreeTime

1. Swipe down from the top of the screen to access the Quick Actions panel, and then tap **Settings**.
2. Tap on **Profiles & Family Library**.
3. Tap **Add a child profile**. Note that if you have not done so before, you may need to set up a lock screen PIN/password in order for your child to use Amazon FreeTime.
4. Select **Choose a profile picture** to add a profile picture.
5. Enter your child's name, birth date, and gender, and then select between **Blue Sky Theme** (for kids under 9 years old)

or **Midnight Black Theme** (for children ages nine and older).

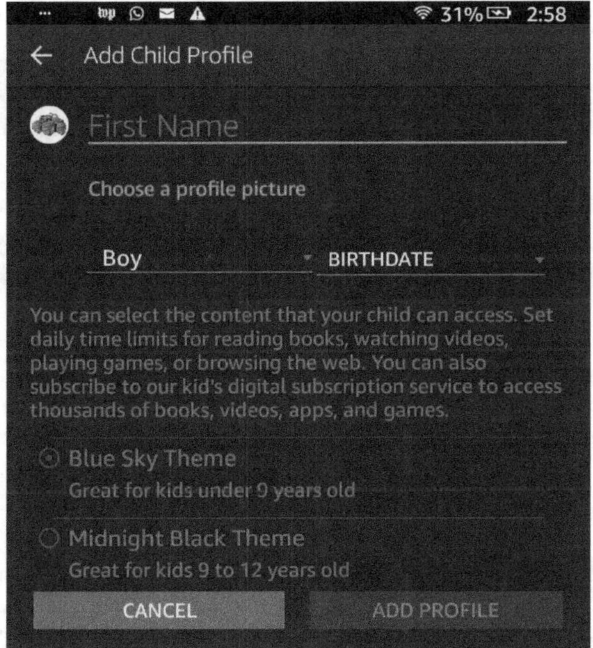

6. Tap **Add Profile**.

7. Tap each content category and select the titles you want to add to your child profile. Tap **Done** to save all the settings. If you don't see the option to select contents, please refer to the section below on page 107 to know how to add contents.

8. If a screen appears prompting you to disable the web browser, tap **Disable Browser** to disable web browsing.

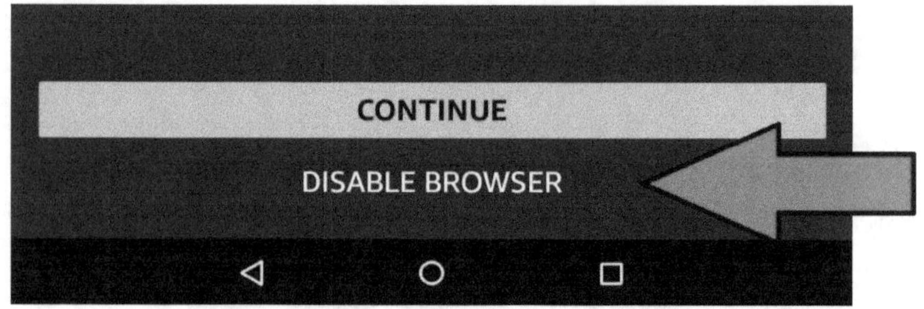

To manage your child profile afterward, go to **Settings** > **Profiles & Family Library**. Then tap on the name of the child you want to manage.

Hint: To access your child's profile after you have set it up, swipe down from the top of the screen to access Quick Actions panel. Then select your profile picture and select the profile of your child from the options that appear.

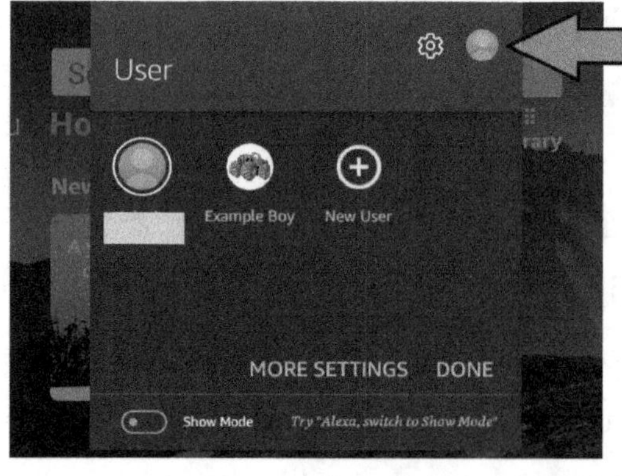

Select your profile picture and then select the profile of your child from the options that appear

How to manage Amazon FreeTime Profile

1. Swipe down from the top of the screen to access the Quick Actions panel, and then tap **Settings**.

2. Tap on **Profiles & Family Library** and tap your child's name.

3. Tap on **Daily Goals & Time Limits**.

4. Tap the status switch next to **Daily Goals & Time Limits**.

Then adjust the following settings as you like:

a) **Weekdays / Weekends**: Use this option to choose different educational goals and time limits for the weekend or weekday.

b) **Bedtime**: Use this option to set a time limit for when your child can use Amazon FreeTime during the day. Use the **Turn off by** setting to set the time when Amazon FreeTime is turned off. Use the **Stay off until** setting to set the time when Amazon FreeTime can be used again.

c) **Educational Goals**: Use this option to set goals for viewing educational content. Use the dropdown menus to choose the amount of time you want your child to view contents. Tap the checkbox next to **Learn First** to prevent non-educational content from being used until your child's goals are met.

d) **Total Screen Time**: Use this option to limit the total time your child can spend in Amazon FreeTime.

e) **Time by Activity**: Use this option to specify individual time limits for specific activities done while using Amazon FreeTime. To choose an unlimited time, move the bar to the far right. To block access to particular content, move the bar to the far left.

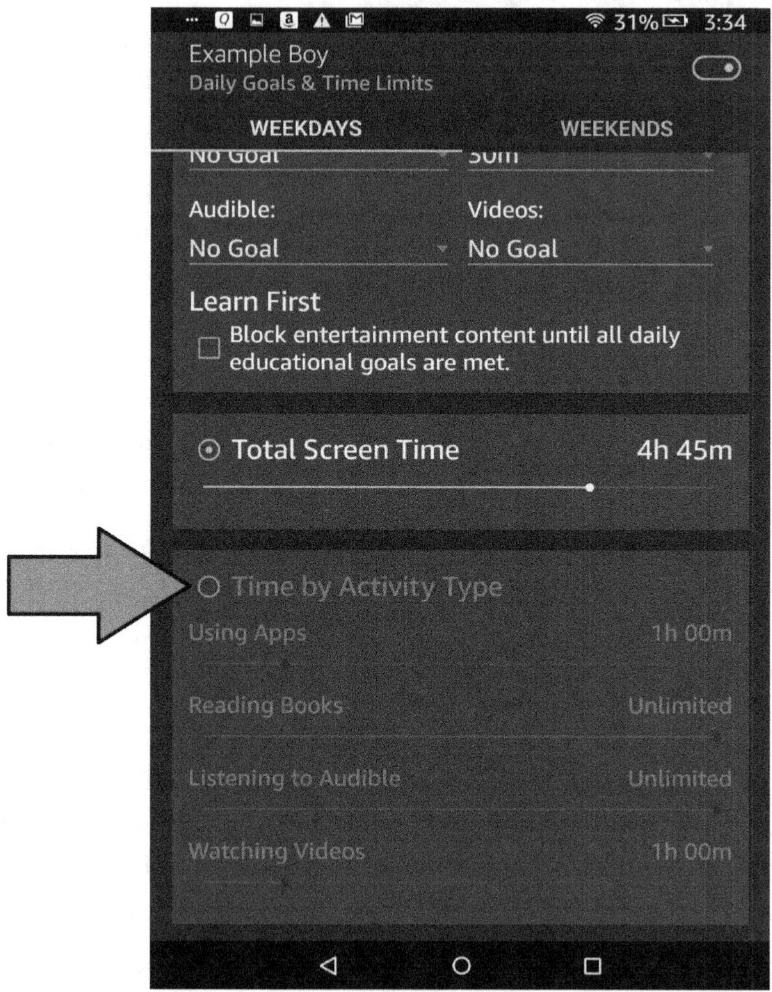

How to add your content to a profile in Amazon FreeTime

One of the beauties of Amazon FreeTime is that you can add exactly what you want to include in your child's profile. You have the option to add books, audiobooks, videos, and apps to your child profile.

To add content to a profile:

1. Swipe down from the top of the screen to access the Quick Actions panel, and then tap **Settings** 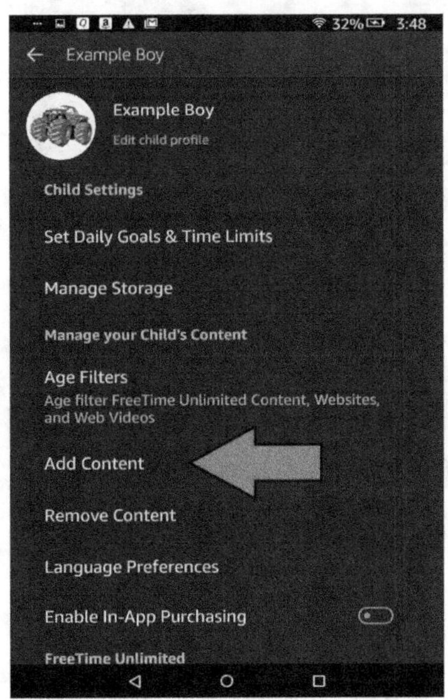.

2. Tap on **Profiles & Family Library** and tap your child's name.

3. Tap **Add Content** and select a content type.

4. Under each category, select the items/titles you want by checking them. You may also remove a title by unchecking the title.

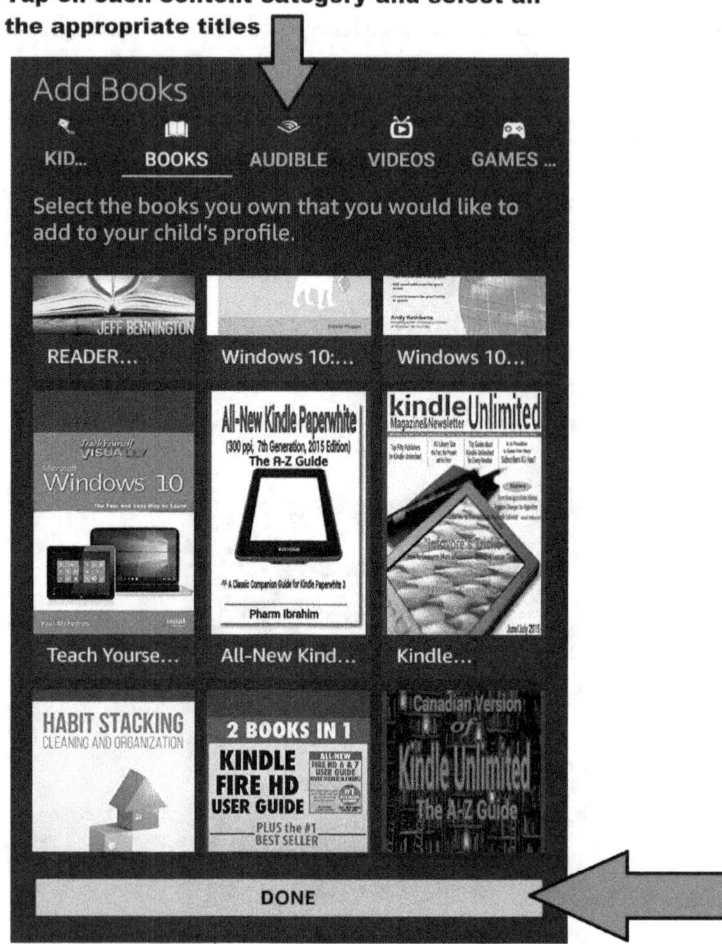

5. Tap **Done.**

Notes:

1. Not all books may be added to a child's profile. Personal documents, audiobooks, Prime videos, and music may not be

added to a profile. However, Amazon made it known that public library books or books borrowed from the Kindle Owner's Lending Library or from Kindle Unlimited can be added to a child's profile. But these books will be unavailable in your child's profile when they are returned or removed from your library.

2. Removing a book from a child's library does not remove it from your device unless you remove the book by selecting **Remove from Device** option.

Using a Profile in Amazon FreeTime

1. To launch a profile, open the Amazon FreeTime app and tap on the profile you want to open. If you are in a lock screen, tap the profile icon in the upper right corner of the screen and then tap the profile you want to open. Then swipe up from the bottom of the screen.

2. To Exit Amazon FreeTime, from the child's profile, swipe down from the top of the screen and tap **Exit Profile.**

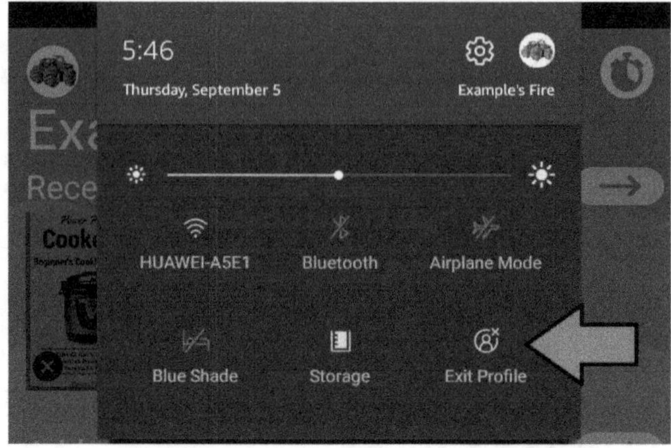

3. To open a title, from the child's profile Home screen, tap a title to open it.

4. To search for content in a child's profile, tap on the search icon found at the top of the screen and then enter a search phrase.

5. To pin an item as favorite, tap and hold the item and select **Add to Favorites.** Pinning favorite items makes it easier to find an item on Home screen.

6. To track the daily progress of a child, from the child profile Home screen, tap the progress icon (found at the top of the screen). This enables you to see how much time your child has left to complete their reading goal, and how much time left until **Bedtime** will appear.

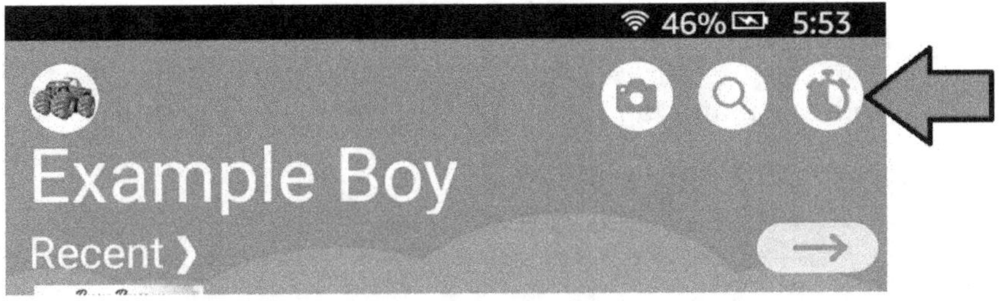

7. To navigate contents, swipe left or right.

8. To go back to your profile and exit the child profile, swipe down from the top of the screen and select the profile picture of your child. Select your profile from the option that appears. Enter your PIN. Press the Home button to go back to your Home screen.

9. To go back to your child profile again, swipe down from the top of the screen and select your profile picture. Select the profile of your child from the options that appear.

Select your child's profile picture and then select your profile from the options that appear

Hint: By default, your child is allowed to take pictures using the camera on your tablet, to disable this option:

1. Swipe down from the top of the screen to access the Quick Actions panel, and then tap **Settings**.

2. Tap on **Profiles & Family Library** and tap your child's profile.

3. Scroll down and tap the status switch next to **Enable Camera & Photo Gallery**.

Editing a Profile

1. Swipe down from the top of the screen to access the Quick Actions panel, and then tap **Settings** .

2. Tap on **Profiles & Family Library** and tap the child's profile name you want to edit.

3. Next to the profile picture of the child, tap **Edit child profile.**

Removing a Profile

4. To remove a child's profile, swipe down from the top of the screen to access the Quick Actions panel, and then tap **Settings** .

5. Tap on **Profiles & Family Library** and tap the child's profile name you want to remove.

6. Scroll down and tap on **Remove Child Profile** and tap **Remove Profile.**

Understanding Amazon Household and Family Library

Amazon Household is a feature that allows you to have joint Amazon account with another adult. This allows you to jointly manage up to four Amazon FreeTime child profiles. Amazon Household typically comprises two adults and up to four children. Amazon Household is accompanied by a feature called Family Library which lets you share books with each other across Amazon devices and Kindle apps.

Note: Your annotations, most recent page read, and the last page read in books are not affected when you share books with other Household members. That is, each adult will keep separate furthest page read locations, notes, highlights, and social media accounts.

To set-up or add an adult to your household:

1. Swipe down from the top of the screen to access the Quick Actions panel, and then tap **Settings** .

2. Tap on **Profiles & Family Library** and tap **Add a second adult profile**.

3. Sign in to your account if needed.

4. You will then need to give your device to the adult you want to add to your household to enable him/her to enter his/her Amazon account details. You may not need to give your device to the other individual if you know his/her account details. If the other individual does not have an Amazon

account, then that person must create one by visiting Amazon website in order to continue the set-up process.

5. After entering the account details, the person will have the option to choose what to share. Note that when the person you are adding chooses to enable sharing, he/she is authorizing you to use credit cards associated with his/her Amazon account for purchase on Amazon. It is important that you explain this information to whoever you are adding to avoid any unnecessary surprises.

6. Carefully follow the onscreen instructions to complete the setup.

Note:

- Family library will not be set up if either adult (i.e. you or the second adult) declines to enable content sharing. However, the second adult may still be added to your household and the management of child profiles with Amazon FreeTime may be shared with the two adults.

To manage which devices can view shared content:

If you enable content sharing, you may be able to choose which device gets access to shared content by following the instructions below:

1. Swipe down from the top of the screen and tap **Settings** , and then tap **Profiles & Family Library**.

2. Tap the partner's profile name, and then tap **Select Devices That Show...... Content.**

3. Then select the devices or Kindle reading apps that you want to allow to access shared content.

Creating a child profile in your household

You can create up to four child profiles in your household and choose which content is shared with them. Note that if you have already created up to four Amazon FreeTime child profiles as described in the preceding section, then you may skip these steps because they should be automatically added to your Household. Creating a child profile in your household on your device is similar to what was described in the preceding section.

To create a child profile in your household from the Amazon website:

1. Launch www.amazon.com/mycd from your browser.

2. Click on **Preferences/Settings** tab, and locate **Households and Family Library**.

3. From Households and Family Library, click on **Add Child**.

4. Follow the onscreen instructions to complete the processs.

Removing an Account from Household

For one reason or the other, you may choose to remove an adult account from your household. However, if you remove an adult account from household or an adult voluntarily leaves your household, neither you nor the second adult may be able to link another adult account or join another household within a period of 180 days.

To remove an adult account from your household:

1. Swipe down from the top of the screen to access the Quick Actions panel, and then tap **Settings** .

2. Tap on **Profiles & Family Library** and tap the adult's profile you want to remove.

3. Tap on **Remove from household.**

To remove an adult account from your household on Amazon website:

1. Launch www.amazon.com/mycd from your browser.

2. Click on **Preferences/Settings** tab, and locate **Households and Family Library**.

3. From Households and Family Library, locate the adult profile you want to remove and hover the mouse over it or click on it (if necessary), and then click **Leave Household** or **Remove from household** from the options. Then click on **Remove Adult**.

Note that child profiles are unaffected by the removal of an adult account from a household. Child profiles will remain with the account that did not leave the household. To delete a child's profile, please follow the instructions on page 112.

In addition, most settings on your Fire tablet only affects your profile, however, settings like Wi-Fi, language, date and time, and parental controls may affect all the profiles on your device.

A Comprehensive Guide on Reading Books on Your Device

One of the top things you will probably be using your tablet to do is reading, and we will like to really talk about it at length in this section.

Reading a book

To read a book:

1. Tap on the book app on the Home screen.
2. To read any book from your library, tap on it.
3. To search for more books, swipe in from the left edge of the screen and select **Store**. Use the search bar found at the top of the screen to search for books.

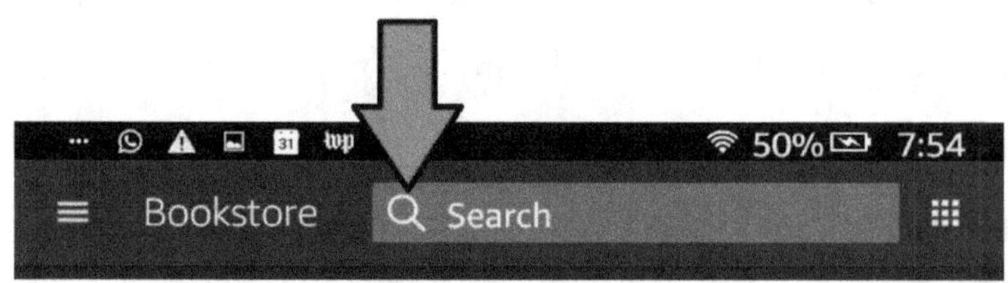

To move out of Amazon bookstore, tap the back icon until you see your book library.

4. Swipe in from left edge of the screen to access left panel to navigate menus.

5. When reading a book, you may move between pages by swiping your finger across the screen.

To change the fonts, margins, line spacing, or background color of a book:

1. While on a page of the book you want to read, tap on the center of the screen to bring out the toolbar.

2. Then tap on **Aa** icon located upper part of the screen.

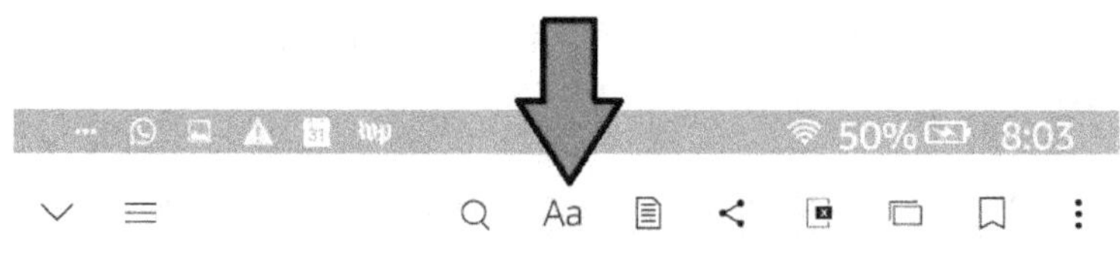

Then do the following:

a. To adjust the screen brightness, drag the slider to right or left.

b. To change the font size, tap + or – next to **Font Size.**

c. To change the font, tap the current font name and then select a font. If available, you may also select publisher font. Not all books support this.

d. To change the background color, tap the small drop-down arrow next to **Color** and then select a color.

e. To change the margins, tap the small drop-down arrow next to **Margins,** and choose from the available options.

f. To change the line spacing, tap the small drop-down arrow next to **Line Spacing,** and pick the line spacing of your choice.

g. When you are done, tap the outside of the dialog box.

Navigating pages of a book

To go to the next or previous page in a book:

1. Open the book of your choice by tapping on the cover or the title of the book from the books app home page.

2. Tap the right side of the screen to go to the next page or tap the left side of the screen to go to the previous page.

3. Alternatively, you may swipe towards left with your finger to go to the next page or swipe toward the right to go to the previous page.

4. To quickly move through pages, tap the center of the screen to bring the reading progress bar into view and then drag the small circle on the reading progress bar to quickly move across different pages of the book. The reading progress bar is the long bar at the lower part of the screen that shows your location in a book and the percentage of the book you have read.

5. To show the current time while reading a book, tap the center of the book you are reading to bring out the reading toolbar. Then tap the menu icon located at the top left corner of the screen and select **Additional Settings.**

Tap the status switch next to **Show Clock While Reading**.

Tap the back icon to navigate back to the book you are reading.

Syncing to the furthest page read

While reading a book, you can sync to the furthest page read across your device by swiping in from the left edge of the screen. Then select **Sync**.

X-Ray feature

X-Ray allows you to get more information about the book you are reading. With X-Ray feature, you can view notable clips, images, terms and people right from the page you are in a book. This feature allows you to see all the passages in a book that mention a particular term, places, topics, historical figures, and more.

Downside: Unfortunately, this feature is not available in all books present on Amazon. In fact, several thousands of books on Amazon don't have this feature enabled. If you want to know whether a book has X-Ray enabled or not, go to the product description of the book on the Kindle store.

To access the X-Ray feature:

1. When you are on a particular page of a book, press and hold on a character's name or place mentioned to bring out the smart lookup card.

2. If the X-Ray is available for the book, you should see X-Ray results displayed alongside the Wikipedia and Dictionary results on the smart lookup card. You may need to swipe left or right to move across the cards. To get access to more X-Ray information, tap on **Go to X-Ray**.

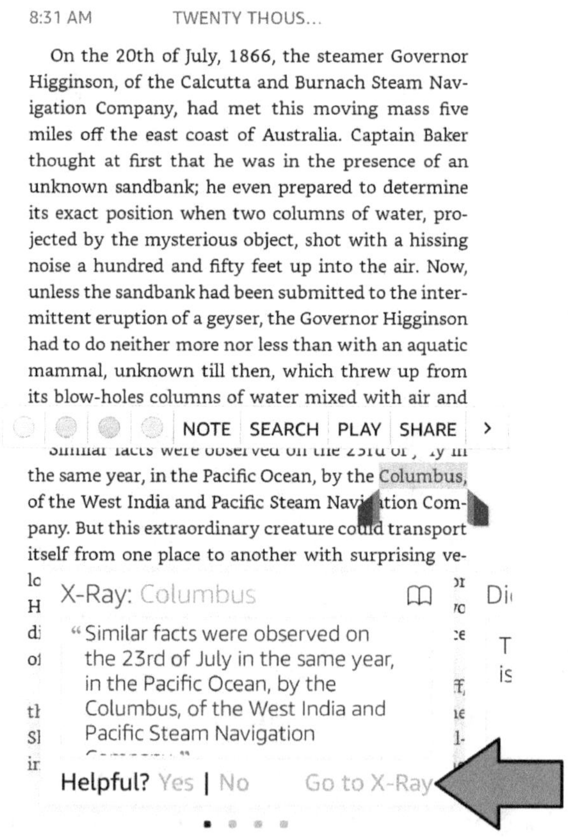

Hint: If you come across a new term, name of a person or place, then try checking if there is X-Ray result for it. This allows you to see different locations in the book containing that particular term or name of a place. To check any word for X-Ray, follow the step mentioned above.

To get access to more comprehensive X-Ray results while reading, please follow the steps below:

1. While reading, tap the center of the screen to display the reading toolbar.
2. Then tap on the X-Ray icon.

3. If the book has the X-Ray enabled, then a dialog box will appear. Generally, the dialog box should contain the X-Ray results for people, places, terms, images, and notable clips.

Note that it may be just three tabs in some cases, because the image tab may be missing in books that have no image in them.

The X-Ray tabs are explained below:

i.   Notable Clip: This tab contains notable passages/scenes in a book

ii.   People: This tab generally includes the names of people featured in the book. Under this tab, you can sort your X-Ray results by Relevance or Alphabetically.

iii.   Term: This tab typically contains the names of places, historical figures, etc. Under this tab, you can sort your X-Ray results by Relevance or Alphabetically.

iv.   Image: This tab allows you to flip through the images in a book.

While reading any book that supports X-Ray feature, tap on any tab mentioned above to check the details under each of them.

Blue Shade

Blue shade gives a characteristic color to the screen of your tablet. When used at night, this feature suppresses the amount of blue light emitted by Fire tablets. This feature is claimed to make sleeping easier after a night reading.

To turn Blue Shade on/off:

- Swipe down from the top of the screen and tap **Blue Shade**.

To adjust Blue Shade settings:

- Swipe down from the top of the screen and select Settings.

- Tap **Display**, and then tap **Blue Shade**. Use the slider bar under **Color** to adjust the Blue Shade.

- Turn on **Automatic Activation** if you want Blue Shade to automatically turn on in the evening and automatically off at sunrise.

Sharing a Text/Passage

You can share what you are reading with friends by using the Share button. Using this sharing feature makes it very easy to quickly share a book with loved ones so that they can also get a copy of the book. This is because a link to the book is usually automatically included when you share a portion of a book.

To share a note or a highlight:

1. Tap, hold and drag to select what you want to share, and then choose **Share** from the dialog box that appears.

2. Follow the onscreen instruction to complete this process.

Bookmarking a Page

You can bookmark those pages of a book that interest you most. You may also use the bookmark feature to know the place you stopped reading.

To bookmark a page:

1. While on the page you want to bookmark, tap the center of the screen to bring reading tool icons into view.

2. Tap the bookmark icon.

3. Select **Add Bookmarks**.

4. To remove the bookmark, repeat steps 1 and 2 above, tap the bookmark you want to remove and select **Remove Bookmark**.

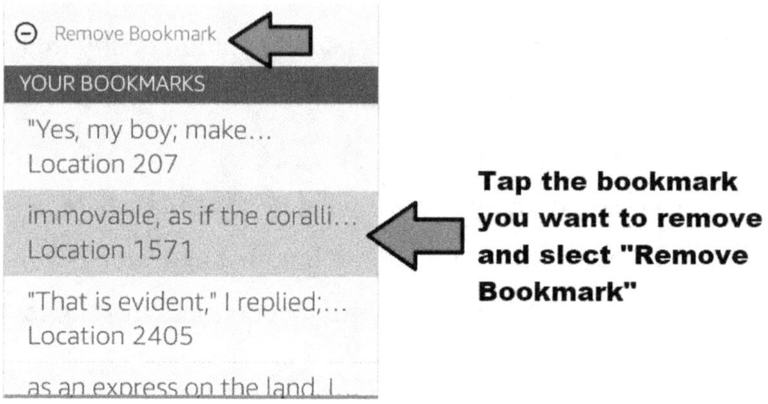

5. To manage your bookmarks, tap the center of the screen to bring the reading toolbar into view, and then tap the **Bookmarks** icon .

Hint: When a page is bookmarked, you would see a bookmark badge at the top right corner of the page.

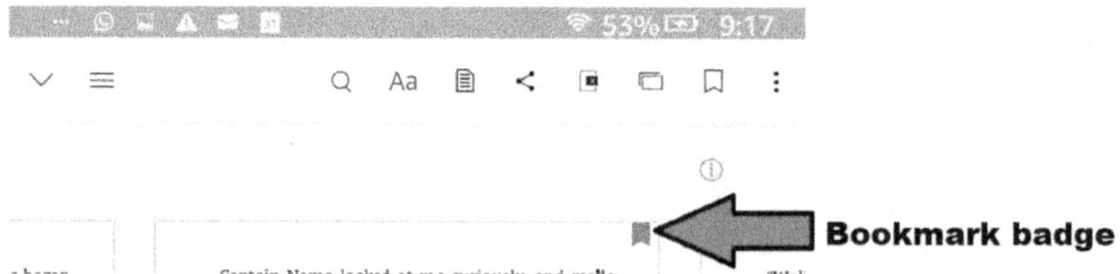

Managing highlights

Just as we use a marker to shade interesting passages in a book, you can also shade those passages in a book that are important to you by highlighting them.

To highlight a text/passage:

1. While reading a book, tap and drag across the words you want to highlight.

2. Choose a color.

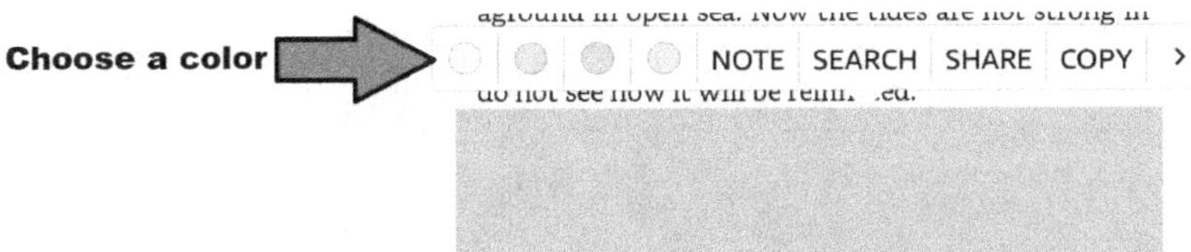

Tip: If you want to highlight a large passage that runs into another page, tap and drag across the words you want to highlight, the page will automatically turn when you get to the bottom right corner of the screen. You can continue like this to select more pages of a book.

To delete your highlights in a book:

1. Open the book and locate the highlight you want to delete.

2. Press and hold a word in the highlighted area, tap **X** icon located on the color previously selected.

Hints: To edit a highlight, follow the above steps to delete the highlight and then reselect appropriate text you want to include in the highlight and tap on a color.

To change the highlight color, press and hold a word in the highlighted area and select another color from the dialog box that appears.

To turn on/off Popular Highlights:

1. Tap the center of the screen to bring the reading toolbar into view, and then tap the menu icon ⋮ located at the upper right corner of the screen.

2. Tap **Additional Settings**.

3. Tap the switch next to **Popular Highlights** to turn it on or off.

Hint: Popular highlights are usually marked by dashed underline. You can check for this when reading.

Managing notes

Notes are the text you type, this is similar to jotting notes in the margins of a printed book.

To add a note to a text/passage:

1. While reading a book, tap and drag across the words you want to add a note to.

2. Tap **Note**, and then type your note.

3. Tap **Save** to create your note. A small notepad appears in the text where you made the note.

To edit your notes:

1. Tap the notepad icon 🗒.

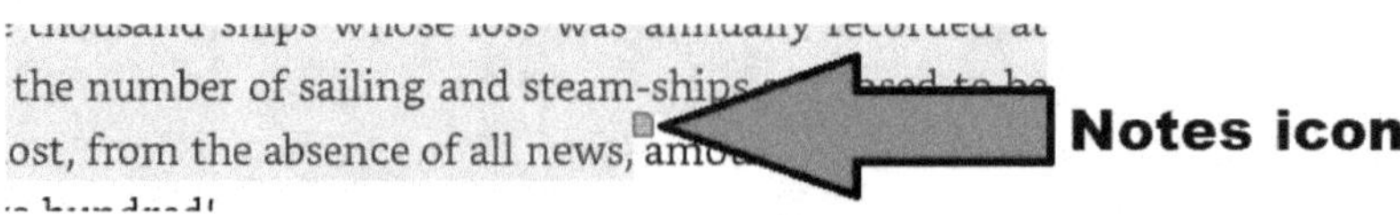

2. Make the necessary changes.

3. Tap **Save** when you are done.

To delete your notes in a book:

1. Tap the notepad icon .
2. Tap **Delete**. Tap **Delete** again to confirm,

Dictionary

The language you choose when setting up your device may determine the dictionary that shows up when using your device. However, you may change your default language at any time. Please note that changing the Language of your device may also change the default dictionary language. To learn more about changing the device language, please refer to page 16.

To access the Dictionary:

1. While reading a book, tap and hold on a word and swipe right (if necessary) until the Dictionary dialogue box is brought into view.
2. Tap **Full Dictionary** to see more information about the word you are viewing.
3. Tap **Change Dictionary** to select another dictionary.

Please note that you may be asked to download a dictionary before you can use it.

Wikipedia

Your device comes with the Wikipedia feature. This feature allows you to look up words in Wikipedia (an online free encyclopedia).

To access Wikipedia:

1. While reading a book, tap and hold on a word and swipe right or left (if necessary) until the Wikipedia tab appears.

2. To learn more about the word or phrase, tap **Go to Wikipedia.**

Translation

You can translate words from one language to another on your device.

1. While reading a book, tap and hold a word and swipe right or left until the Translation tab appears.

2. To change the Language you want to translate to, tap on it.

3. To hear the translated text, tap the speaker button.

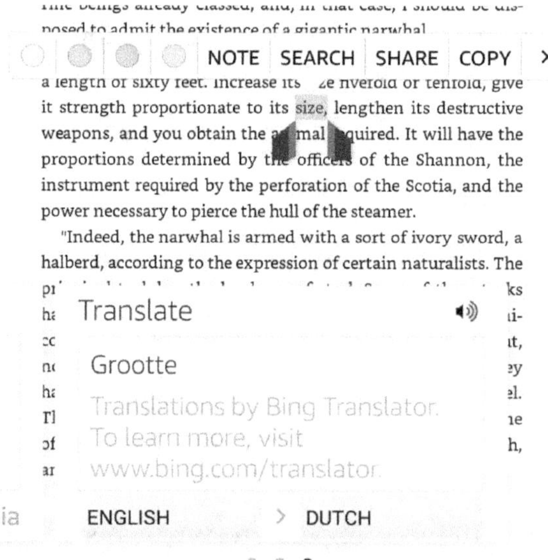

Using the Flashcards

You can access flashcards when reading some books (textbooks).

1. Tap the center of the book to bring the reading toolbar into view.

2. Tap the flashcard icon.

3. To create flashcards, tap + icon (found at the middle or top of the screen) and enter a name for your Flashcard. Then tap the checkmark found at the top of the screen to save changes.

4. Tap on **Front** and enter the question. Tap **Back** and enter the answer. Then tap on the checkmark found at the top right part of the screen to save the changes.

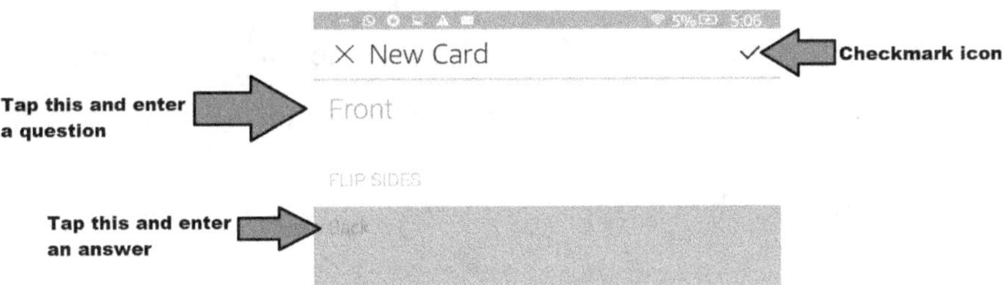

5. To add more cards to a flashcard, tap the plus icon located at the top of the screen.

Then tap on the checkmark ✓ found at the top right part of the screen to save the changes.

6. To edit flashcards, tap and hold the flashcard you want to edit and select the pen icon ✎ . Then tap the card you want to edit and enter the necessary changes. Tap the checkmark icon ✓ to save the changes.

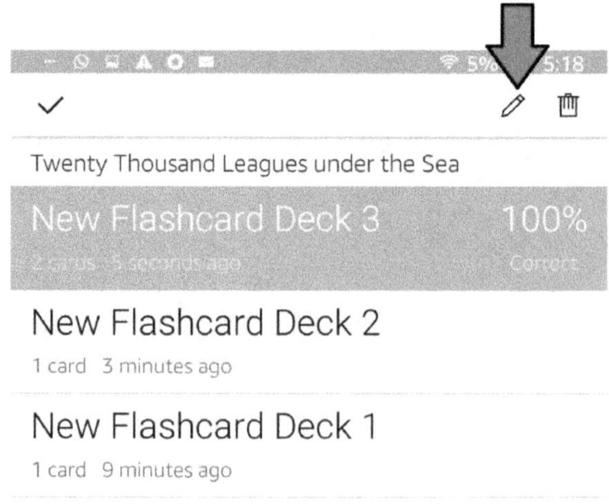

7. To delete flashcards, tap and hold the flashcard you want to delete and select the delete icon 🗑 .

In a flashcard that contains multiple cards, you can delete a single card instead of deleting the whole flashcard. To do this, tap and hold the flashcard containing the card you want to delete and then select the pen icon ✎ . Tap the card you want to delete. Then tap on the menu icon ⋮ found at the top of the screen and select **Delete**.

8. To study a flashcard, tap the flashcard and then tap a card in the flashcard. Answer the question shown to you. Tap the card again to read the information on the other side of the card. If the answer is correct, select **Correct** ✓ , if not, select **Incorrect** ✕ .

9. To reshuffle a set, tap ⤨ icon.

10. To restart a set, tap ↻ icon.

Word Wise

Word Wise feature on your Fire tablet makes it easy to view meanings of complex words without the need to look words up. This feature is really beneficial for small kids. It also makes learning old English words easier.

Downside: Not all books have Word Wise enabled. You can know if a book has a Word Wise feature enabled by checking the product description page of the book in the Kindle store.

To turn on or turn off Word Wise:

1. While reading a book, tap the center of the screen to bring the reading toolbar into view, and then tap the menu icon ⋮ in the upper right corner of the screen.
2. Tap the indicator switch next to **Word Wise** to enable it. To disable it, tap it again.

To manage Word Wise

When Word Wise feature is on for an enabled title, your device automatically displays simple meanings of difficult words. Tap on any of these words to learn more about them. In addition, you can tap on the **Word Wise** icon found at the bottom of the screen and adjust the number of Word Wise hints you see.

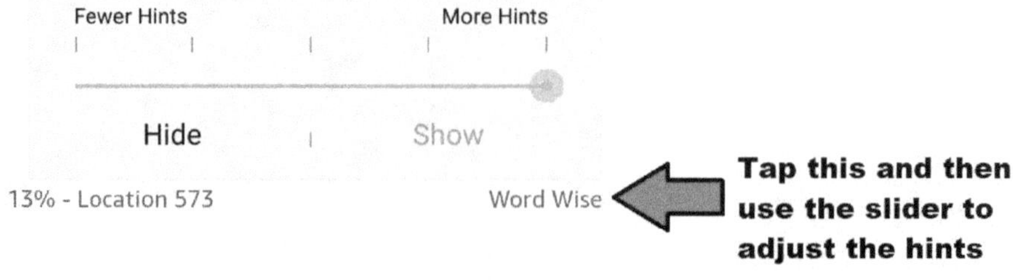

Using the Word Runner

Word runner allows you to read books without moving your look. With this feature, you can easily fix your look at the center of the screen.

To use Word Runner:

1. Tap the center of the screen to bring the reading toolbar into view, and then tap the menu icon ⋮ in the upper left corner.

2. Tap **Word Runner.**

3. Tap the play icon ▶ located at the bottom of the page you are reading.

4. Use the slider at the button of the screen to adjust the speed of Word Runner. You can choose between 50 to 900 words per minute.

5. To pause Word Runner to quickly do some things, tap and hold the current word. To continue using Word Runner, just remove your finger from the word. You can also tap on the pause icon ❚❚ to pause this feature. When you are done, tap on the play icon ▶ .

6. To reread a sentence while using Word Runner, tap the pause icon ▐▐ , and then tap the forward ↻ or backward ↺ icon to move through sentences. When you are done, tap the play button to continue reading at the new location.

7. To exit Word Runner, tap the **X** icon (found at the top left edge of the screen) and then tap the arrow icon ← located at the top left corner of the screen.

Please note that you may not be able to view images while using Word Runner. It appears that images are not supported on Word Runner. Maybe this will be supported in the future. You can tap the **X** icon to quickly view images in a book while using Word Runner.

Using Text-to-Speech

If you don't have the audiobook of a book but you have an eBook version, you can try using the text-to-speech feature.

You can know if a book has the Text-to-Speech feature enabled by checking the product description page of the book in Kindle store.

To use the Text-to-Speech feature:

1. Tap the center of the screen to bring the reading toolbar into view, and then tap the menu icon ⁞ located at the upper right corner of the screen.

2. Tap **Additional Settings.**

3. Tap the switch next to **Text-to-Speech**. Tap the back button ◁ to navigate back to the book.

4. While reading the book, tap the center of the screen to bring the reading toolbar into view, and then tap on play icon 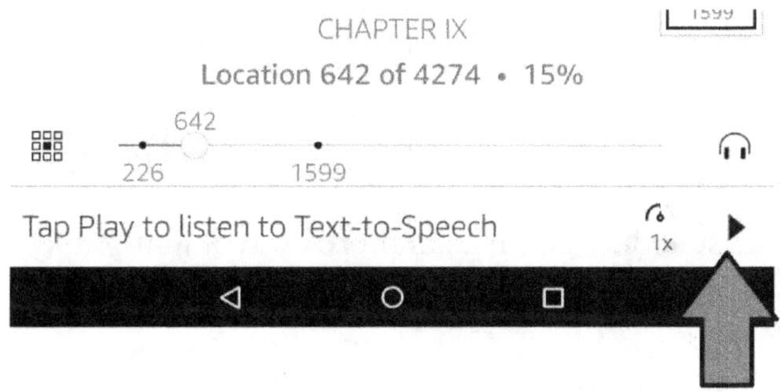 .

5. To adjust the reading speed, tap the speed icon .

6. If you are reading a book in another language, you may have the option to download the Text-to-Speech voice for this language.

Creating schedules and more with the Calendar

Your tablet provides you with the **Calendar** app to help you organize your schedules and tasks more conveniently and effectively. You can create schedules and add events.

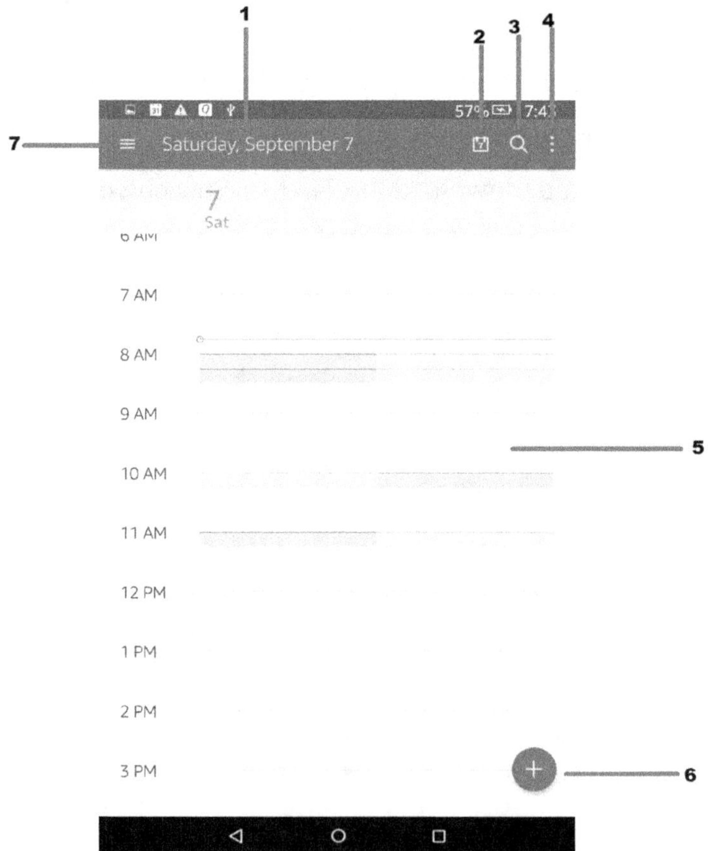

Number	Function
1.	Date field
2.	Day view icon
3.	Use this icon to search your calendar
4.	Menu icon: Use this to access agenda, day view, week view or month view
5.	Time/Day field
6.	Tap this icon to add an event
7.	Tap this to bring out the left panel

Creating an event

1. Open the application grid and tap on the **Calendar** app .

2. Tap on the '+' icon at the right lower side of the screen and enter the details.

3. When you are finished, tap checkmark ✓ (found at the top of the screen) to save the event.

Changing the calendar view

1. Open the application grid and tap on the **Calendar** app.

2. Tap the menu icon ⋮ (found at the top of the screen) to switch between **Agenda, Day, Week and Month Views**.

Viewing an event/schedule

1. Open the application grid and tap on the **Calendar** app.

2. If the calendar is set to display the **Day** view, the calendar app automatically displays the events for the day.

3. Tap on an event to view.

Editing or deleting an event

1. Open the application grid and tap on **Calendar**.

2. If the calendar is set to display the **Day** view, the calendar app automatically displays the events for the day.

3. Tap the event.

4. Tap the menu icon ⁝ (found at the top of the screen) and then tap the **Edit** icon.

5. To delete an event, tap the event and then tap the **Delete** icon .

Viewing and Hiding Your Calendars

If you have multiple calendars (calendars from Yahoo mail, Facebook, etc.) synced to your tablet you can select which ones to display.

1. Open the application grid and tap on the **Calendar** app .

2. Swipe in from the left edge of the screen, and then tap the checkbox next to the calendar (item) you want to display.

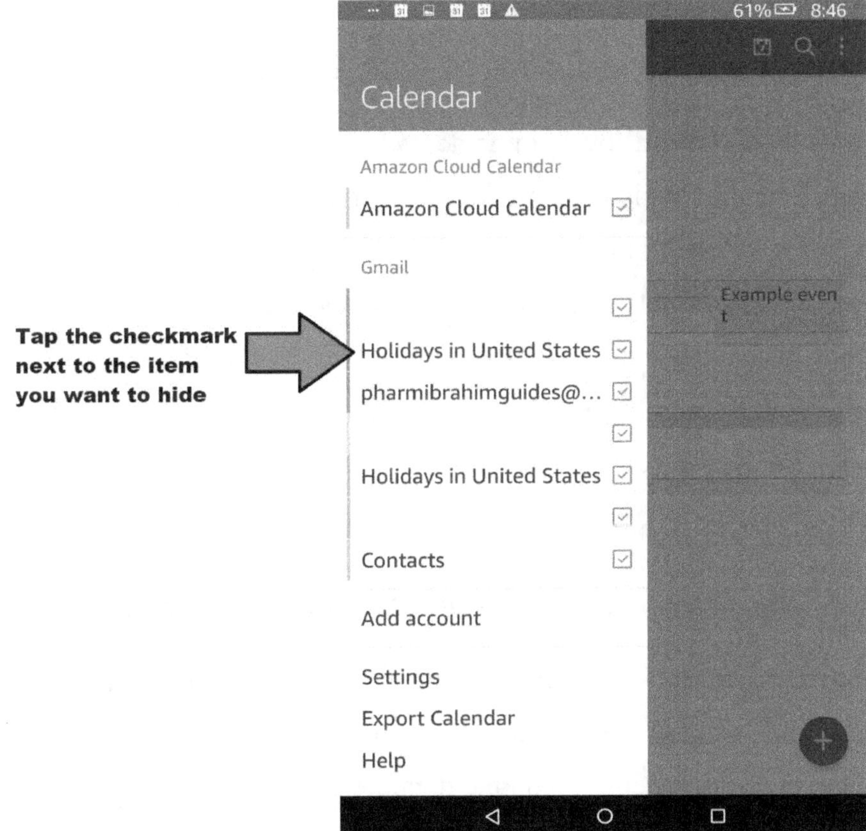

Hint: To customize your calendar even more, swipe from the left edge of the screen and tap on **Settings.**

Managing your document with Docs App

Docs is an app that allows you to access documents present on your tablet. You should also be able to view documents that you transfer from your PC under this app.

Note: Not all formats of documents are supported. The supported document formats include PDF, unprotected MOBI, PRC natively, DOC, DOCX, Kindle (AZW), KF8, TXT

> **To access your documents**

1. From the Home screen, tap on **DOCS** on the app grid.

2. To delete or send a document using email, tap the menu icon next to the document and select an appropriate option.

3. To view a document, tap on the document you want to view.

Hint: To enjoy viewing large pdf files, I will advise you to download the official PDF application from Amazon Appstore. Besides, **WPS Office + PDF** app is good for viewing and editing documents and you may consider downloading it from Amazon Appstore.

To learn more about how to send a document to your device using the Send-to-Kindle option, please refer to page 183-186.

Using the Camera

Fire tablets come with both rear-facing camera and front-facing cameras. With these cameras, you can capture a photo or record a video.

Note: The memory capacity of the picture taken may differ depending on the shooting scene and shooting conditions.

Hint: When enabled, both photos and videos can be backed up automatically on the cloud when on Wi-Fi.

To disable/enable this feature, open the **Amazon Photos** app  and tap on the **More** icon More found at the bottom of the screen. Then tap **Settings** and tap **Auto-Save**. Tap the switch next to Photos/Videos.

Depending on the Fire tablet you are using, please note that some of the features mentioned below may not be supported on your device.

> ➤ **To Capture a photo**

1. Open the application grid and select the **Camera**.

2. Aim the lens at the subject and make any necessary adjustments. To focus any part of the screen, tap that part of the screen.

3. Tap **front-facing/rear-facing icon** to switch between the rear-facing and front-facing camera.

4. To zoom in, place two fingers on the screen and spread them apart. Do the reverse to zoom out.

5. Tap on the **shutter button** to take a photo. To capture many photos, press and hold the shutter button.

6. After taking photos, you may select the image viewer to view the photos. To exit the image viewer, tap on image viewer icon again.

Customizing the Camera Settings

1. Repeat step 1 above.

2. Tap on the setting icon and tap a setting.

Recording a video

1. From the Home screen, select the **Camera**.

2. Aim the lens at the subject and make any necessary adjustments. To focus any part of the screen, tap that part of the screen.

3. Tap on the **video button** to start recording.

4. To zoom in while recording, place two fingers on the screen and spread them apart. To zoom out, move the two fingers closer together.

5. When done with the recording, tap the **video button** 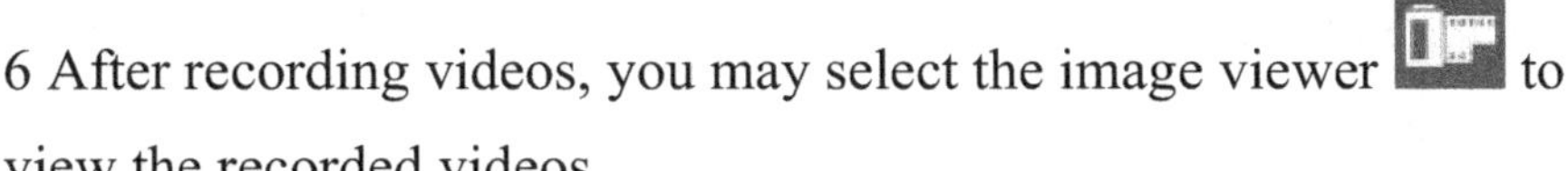 again.

6 After recording videos, you may select the image viewer to view the recorded videos.

Hint: To capture pictures while recording a video, tap the **shutter icon** 

Note: If the feature is enabled, both the photos and the videos on your tablet are automatically backed up on the Amazon server when connected to Wi-Fi. Please go to the beginning of this chapter to learn how to enable automatic backup.

Editing Your Photos

You can use your tablet to edit photos.

1. Open the app grid and tap on **Amazon Photos**. Alternatively, you may access your photos by tapping the **Image Viewer** located on your camera screen.

2. Tap on the photo you want to edit.

3. Then tap on the menu icon ⋮ and then select the **Edit icon**. Select the editing tool of your choice.

4. To delete a photo, tap on the menu icon ⋮ and then select **Move to Trash** button .

Viewing your photos

1. Open the app grid and tap on **Amazon Photos** .
2. Tap a photo to view.
3. While on the Amazon Photos Home screen, press and hold a photo to activate the selection tool in order to select multiple photos to share, delete or upload to the cloud.

Getting Productive With the Camera

Many people use the camera of their tablet just to take pictures, but don't know that they can be using their tablet camera for more productive tasks.

In this section, we will be exploring ways we can be more productive with our tablet's camera.

Ways to be more productive with your tablet's camera are mentioned below:

- **Use your tablet camera as a scanner for your documents**

You probably have many documents that are very important to you. Why don't you look for time to take the pictures of all these documents and save them to your Fire tablet or have them stored in the cloud. There are times that you would want to check something inside a document, but you are not at home. Saving your documents on your tablet should help you in a time like this.

In addition, saving documents on your Fire tablet will save you time and stress because you have access to them on the go.

Top Android document scanners include **Microsoft Office Lens** and **Adobe Scan**. You can download their APK files so as to install them on your Fire tablet. Please go to page 176 to learn more about APK.

- **Take pictures of a natural environment like a waterfall and natural vegetation**

According to reports, looking at the images of natural environments like waterfalls and natural vegetations gives people pleasure and serves as coolness to one's eyes. In addition, it helps you appreciate the beautiful works of the Almighty God.

- **Declutter your life**

Do you know that you can use the camera of your tablet to declutter your life? You probably have many hand-written documents, business cards, to-do list, etc. lying all over the place in your home. You can take pictures of these notes so that you can remove them from your house and give them to appropriate waste recycling companies. This will create more space in your house and give you more visual ventilation.

We would advise you properly label the pictures of your hand-written documents, business cards, to-do list, etc. to help you easily find them in the future. In addition, you can consider saving the pictures of your hand-written documents, business cards, to-do list, etc. on *Evernote*. We suggest Evernote because it gives you the opportunity to search texts inside images.

- **Use your camera as a barcode and QR (quick response) code scanner**

Barcode and QR code are machine readable codes that are used to store information. Barcode is linear or one dimensional in nature. It basically looks like a cluster of parallel lines. On the other hand, QR code is two dimensional in nature. An example of a QR code is shown below. Interestingly, your Fire tablet is capable of barcodes and reading QR codes using barcode scanner apps. Many of us still take the long path of entering texts or links when we can get the same result by scanning barcode or QR code.

Example of a QR code

You can install a barcode scanner from Google Play store. Simply search for *barcode scanner* or *QR and barcode scanner.*
To know how to install Google Play store, go to page 190.

- **Take the pictures of notes in meetings and lectures instead of writing them**

Taking the picture of notes after a meeting or a lecture allows you to listen during the meeting or lecture instead of writing notes.

- **Use your camera to take pictures of valuable information/documents in your life**

If you have any valuable piece of information that you can't afford to lose, use your camera to take its picture. That would serve as a backup in case of loss.

Tip: It is a good idea to back up your files/documents on cloud platforms like Dropbox, OneDrive or Google Drive.

Connectivity

PC Connections

Your tablet can be connected to a PC with a USB cable. This will enable you to transfer files such as audio files, video files, document files and image files to your tablet from your PC.

Warning: Do not disconnect the USB cable from a computer while the device is transferring or accessing data. This may result in data loss or damage to your tablet.

Note: Personal content transferred to your Amazon Fire Tablet is stored on your device and may not be stored on the Amazon cloud. However, if your settings permit, image files and video files may be automatically backed up when connected to Wi-Fi.

Transferring content via USB

1. Connect your device to a PC with a USB cable. Your Fire tablet should appear in the same location as external USB drives usually appear. For Windows users, this is typically under "My Computer" or "This PC" menu.

2. Open the Amazon Fire drive so as to see the different folders present. Click on **Internal storage** to see different folders such as **Books**. Note that you may not be able to access the folders if your tablet is locked.

3. To transfer files from your PC to your tablet, locate the file you want to transfer on your PC and click and then drag and drop the file into corresponding folders on your Tablet. For example, books should be dragged to **Books** folder. Alternatively, if you are using a Windows PC, click on the file you want to transfer to the Fire tablet and press **Ctrl + C**. Click on the right folder on your Fire tablet and press **Ctrl + V** to paste.

4. Safely eject your tablet from your PC.

5. Go to Docs app and launch the corresponding content library to see the transferred files.

Note: After the transfer, your transferred files should appear under the corresponding content library on your device:

- Video files should be under Photos

- Image files should be under Photos

- Personal documents should be under Docs library

Note: Note that your tablet will only recognize the files you transferred if the file is a supported file type. We will advise that you download **ES File Explorer** from Amazon Appstore so as to have real-time control of the files on your tablet.

In addition, Mac users will need to download a file transfer app from **www.android.com/filetransfer** in order to be able to transfer files from their computer to Fire tablet.

Note: If you do a factory reset to your tablet, you may need to re-transfer the files again.

Hint: You can download your purchased books to your computer and then transfer it via USB to your Fire tablet by following these steps:

1. Go to **www.amazon.com/mycd**

2. Tap on **My Contents** tab and tap on small action box next to the title you want to download

3. Select **Download & Transfer via USB**

Wi-Fi

Using your tablet, you can connect to the internet or other network devices anywhere an access point or wireless hotspot is available.

To activate the Wi-Fi feature and connect to a network

1. Swipe down from the top of the screen to open the quick actions menu, and then tap **Settings** .

2. Tap on **Wireless & Bluetooth**.

3. Tap on **Wi-Fi**.

4. Tap the switch next to **Wi-Fi** to turn it **on.**

5. You may also manually add a network by tapping the menu

   icon ⋮ and selecting **Add Network**.

6. Select a network under *Wi-Fi networks*.

7. Enter a password for the network (if necessary).

8. Tap **Connect**.

Notes:

- The Wi-Fi feature running in the background will consume battery. To save battery, put it off whenever you are not using it.

- Tap the menu icon ⋮ (the three vertical dots icon located at the top right corner of the screen) to access more Wi-Fi options.

- After you connect to a Wi-Fi network, your device should connect automatically to it again whenever that network is in range.

- The Wi-Fi may not connect a network if the network signal is not very good.

- If your device can't connect to a wireless network, check if the airplane mode is on. If the airplane mode is off and you can't still connect to a wireless network, try restarting your router or your tablet or both.

Tip: To disable all wireless connections, turn **on** the **airplane mode** by swiping down from the top of the screen of your tablet and tapping on the **Airplane Mode**.

When Wi-Fi is active, **Wi-Fi** icon is displayed on the status bar.

Access More By Using Bluetooth

Bluetooth option allows you to connect to another Bluetooth device within range

Note: If there are obstacles, the operating distance of the Bluetooth may be reduced.

To use the Bluetooth feature:

1. Swipe down from the top of the screen to open the quick actions menu, and then tap **Settings** .

2. Tap on **Wireless & Bluetooth**.

3. Tap on **Bluetooth**.

4. Then tap the switch next to **Bluetooth.**

5. Tap **Pair a Bluetooth Device.**

6. Select a device to connect with. Tap **Pair** if needed.

7. When the Bluetooth is enabled, a **Bluetooth icon** will appear on the status bar found at the top of the screen.

Please make sure that the device you are trying to connect with has its Bluetooth turned on and discoverable. If you have a problem connecting a Bluetooth device, try restarting your tablet. You can restart your device by shutting down the Fire tablet and then turning it back on.

The following are the Bluetooth Profiles supported by Amazon tablet.

- Advanced Audio Distribution Profile (A2DP)
- Audio/Video Remote Control Profile (AVRCP)
- Human Interface Device Profile (HID)

- Serial Port Profile (SPP)

Location Services

Enabling location service allows Map, Amazon, and some apps to serve your content related services. More importantly, it allows Amazon to trace your Fire tablet in case of loss.

Note: You may have to activate location service in order to receive information and search the map.

To Activate Find Your Tablet/Location Services:

1. Swipe down from the top of the screen to open the quick actions menu, and then tap **Settings**.
2. Tap on **Wireless & Bluetooth**.
3. Tap on **Location-Based Services**.
4. Tap the status switch next to **Location-Based Services**.

To turn on **Find My Device**:

1. Swipe down from the top of the screen to open the quick actions menu, and then tap **Settings**.
2. Tap on **Device Options**.
3. Tap the switch next to **Find Your Tablet.**
4. If prompted, tap **Enable.**

Find My Device Feature

You can use this feature to locate your tablet if lost. Please note that you would need to enable "Find Your Tablet" feature (following the method above) before you can use the feature.

To find your lost tablet:

1. Visit **www.amazon.com/mycd** and log in to your account.
2. Go to **Devices** tab located at the upper center of the screen (if you are browsing with a desktop).
3. Click on the options tab next to the device you want to find.

4. From the menu that appears, you can perform the following actions:

1. **Deregister:** This option can be used to deregister your tablet.

2. **Remote Alarm:** This option can be used to turn on the alarm so that the tablet can make sound. This may help in locating it. This alarm should last for two minutes.

3. **Find Your Tablet**: This option can be used to access the last known location of your tablet.

4. **Remote Lock:** This will allow you to lock the tablet with a new password so as to prevent unwanted access. You can also include a message to display on the lock screen using this feature.

5. **Remote Factory Reset:** This feature allows you to reset your tablet to factory settings. Only choose this option if you are convinced that you may never find your tablet again. This is because you will no longer be able to track your tablet if you select this option. You may need a battery level of 30% to perform this action.

Note:

- To find your device with this option, you must turn on **Find Your Tablet** feature (see page 155 above) before you misplaced the tablet.

- Your lost tablet must be on and connected to a network to allow Amazon to find your device. According to Amazon, if your lost tablet is off or not connected to a network, Amazon will keep trying to reach your tablet for three days.

An alternative way to find your device:

1. Download and install *Lookout Security & Antivirus*
2. Launch the app and register your account. Then go to the **missing device** tab in order to customize relevant settings.

This app can be used to find your missing tablet. It also protects your tablet from malware and can be used to back up your data.

Settings

Settings menu gives you the opportunity to customize your device as you like.

To access the settings menu

1. Swipe down from the top of the screen to open the quick access menu and then tap on **Settings** .

2. Alternatively, you can tap settings icon from the app grid.

The following are options under the settings tab:

Wireless & Bluetooth

This option allows you to connect to a Wi-Fi network and access the internet or other network devices. It also contains Bluetooth settings. To use options under **Wireless & Bluetooth,** please refer to the section on **Connectivity** (see page 150).

Storage

This option allows you to manage your storage.

To manage your device memory:

1. Swipe down from the top of the screen to open the quick actions menu, and then tap **Settings** .

2. Tap on **Storage** to view available memory.

3. Under the **Internal Storage** tab, you will be able to see the amount of unused space on your tablet.

4. Tap **Internal Storage** to view storage by content category. Tap a content category to see details. To delete an item from the **Miscellaneous** category, tap the category and select the checkbox next to the item you want to remove, and then tap **Remove**. *Please note that you may not be prompted when attempting to remove an item, so be careful when using this option to remove an item from your device.*

5. You can tap on **Archive Now** to see if any of your files qualify for **1-Tap Archive** so as to free up space.

6. Tap on **View Contents** to view the storage space of contents on your device.

7. To view and manage the storage used by household profiles on your device (if you have created one), tap on a profile name. Please note that deleting a file under a profile may make it be permanently deleted from your device.

Managing SD Card Storage

Please refer to page 3 to 6 for more information on this.

Power

This option allows you to manage the power settings on your device.

To view your battery usage

1. Swipe down from the top of the screen to open the quick actions menu, and then tap **Settings**.

2. Tap on **Power** to access battery-related settings.

Smart Suspend

Smart suspend is a feature that suspends wireless when not in use. It helps conserve battery life. This feature can be set to manually or automatically manage your tablet's battery life. By default, this feature may be enabled. To disable this feature:

1. Repeat steps 1 and 2 above.
2. Tap the switch next to **Automatic Smart Suspend**.
3. To schedule Smart Suspend, tap the switch next to **Scheduled Smart Suspend** and pick a time by tapping **Schedule**.

Hint: When this feature is enabled, it tries to guess the best time to off your wireless. However, you may tell it when exactly to off your wireless by tapping on **Scheduled Smart Suspend**.

Display Settings

Display settings affect battery life and you can manage it using this option. To manage your display settings:

1. Swipe down from the top of the screen to open the quick actions menu, and then tap **Settings** ⚙.
2. Tap on **Power**.
3. Tap **Display Settings** and adjust necessary settings under this tab in order to conserve your battery life.

Hint: Choosing a lower time to sleep (e.g five minutes) and choosing lower screen brightness may help conserve battery life. In addition, choosing not to rotate the screen may also help save battery life.

Wireless Settings

Wireless Settings affect battery life and you can manage it using this option. To manage your Wireless Settings:

1. Repeat the first two steps above.
2. Tap **Wireless Settings** and adjust the necessary settings to conserve your battery life.

Note: If you're really concerned about conserving battery life, as a rule, wireless should be off when not in use.

Show Mode

This tab contains the Show Mode related settings. To learn more about Show Mode please go to page 61.

Apps & Games

This feature allows you to manage your applications and game settings.

To configure Amazon application settings:

1. Swipe down from the top of the screen to open the quick actions menu, and then tap **Settings** .

2. Tap on **Apps & Games**.

3. Then tap on **Amazon Application Settings**.

4. Tap on an application to customize its settings.

To manage non-Amazon applications on your device:

1. Repeat steps 1 and 2 above.

2. Tap on **Manage All Applications.**

3. Then tap on the particular application you want to manage from the list of applications. You can use **Downloaded** and **Running** tabs to filter results.

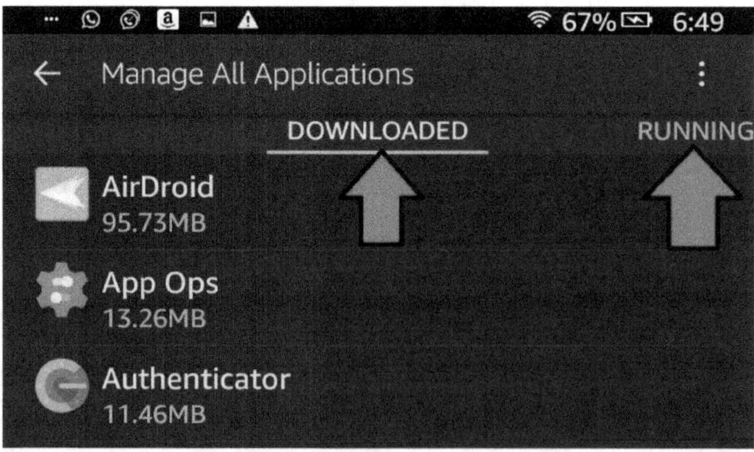

Notes:

- You can use this option to force quit or uninstall an application. You can choose **force stop** if you notice that the app is not behaving properly. This will stop the app from carrying out any process on your tablet. To enable the app again, just launch the app. You may also consider uninstalling the app if you find out that you do not need the app again.

- You also have the option to **clear data, clear cache,** or **clear default** of the app. When you choose **clear data**, all the stored information like settings of the app will be lost but the app will not be uninstalled. This implies that the next time you launch the app, you will be using it as if you are using it for the first time. When you choose **clear cache**, the cache memory is cleared. Cache is a set of data stored on a computer memory so that you can get a faster response when using an item. The **clear default** allows you to clear any default setting you might have stored on the app.

Hint: You can turn on the installation from platforms other than Amazon, please go to page 170 to learn more.

Display

This option allows you to control those aspects of your tablet that has to do with display.

To adjust your screen brightness:

- Please refer to page 22.

To turn off automatic screen rotation

- Please refer to page 8.

To Change the Time to Sleep

You can set your tablet to sleep after a specified time. To effect this, tap on the **Display Sleep** located under **Display** tab, and then set the time of your choice.

To configure font size

Tap on the **Font Size** located under **Display** tab, and then choose a font.

Device

Device settings give you the opportunity to manage many settings associated with your tablet.

Changing the name of your device

1. Swipe down from the top of the screen to open the quick actions menu, and then tap **Settings** .
2. Tap on **Device Options**.

3. Tap on **Change Your Device Name**.

Changing the date and time

- Please refer to page 19.

Find Your Tablet

Please refer to the preceding section on **find my device** (see page 156) to learn more about how to find your device when lost.

Enabling auto backups

It is advisable to back up your tablet to be on a safer side in case of damage or loss. Data from settings, installed apps, bookmarks, and more are backed up.

Note that purchased products such as apps, books, videos, and audios are automatically back up on Amazon cloud.

1. Swipe down from the top of the screen to open the quick actions menu, and then tap **Settings**.
2. Tap on **Device Options**.
3. Tap on **Backup & Restore**.
4. Tap the switch next to **Backup & Restore**.
5. Your tablet will automatically back up once a week when connected to Wi-Fi and it is in standby mode.

Note: If you have backed up your tablet, you will have the opportunity to access your files when you set up a new tablet.

Installing system updates

1. Repeat steps 1 and 2 above.

2. Tap on the **System Updates**.

3. Tap on **Check Now** to install updates.

Please note that installing system updates may sometime make you lose access to some of the tweaks you have done to your device.

Carrying out a Factory Reset

1. Swipe down from the top of the screen to open the quick actions menu, and then tap **Settings** .

2. Tap on **Device Options**.

3. Tap on **Reset to Factory Defaults**.

4. Tap on **Reset**.

When you perform a factory reset on your device, you will still be able to access your items that are backed up in the cloud. Generally, it is recommended you backup (see page 165) your device before you perform a factory reset.

Getting information about your fire tablet

1. Repeat steps 1 and 2 above

2. Scroll down if needed. Your device model is shown under the **Device model** tab while the serial number of your device is shown under the **Serial Number** tab.

My Accounts

This option allows you to manage your account with Amazon and social network accounts.

1.   Swipe down from the top of the screen to open the quick actions menu, and then tap **Settings.**
2.   Tap on the **My Accounts** tab.
3.   Select any of the following options in the list:

A. Deregister: This option allows you to remove the account registered with your tablet and enter another one. You may find this option useful if you find out that a wrong account is linked to your tablet or you wish to change the account to a different one.

B. Amazon account settings: This option gives you the opportunity to manage your Amazon account and customize it. In addition, under this setting, you can choose which payment method to use when you purchase a product from Amazon.

C. Prime Settings: Use this option to view and manage your Prime subscriptions.

D. Social network: This feature gives you the option of customizing your social network accounts. You will able to add/manage social network account under this feature.

Profiles & Family Library

Use these settings to manage your child's profiles and family library. Please go to sections on household profiles (see page 113) and *Amazon FreeTime* (see page 102) to learn more.

Parental Controls

Parental controls

This feature allows you to set up security on some features present on your fire tablet.

To set up parental controls:

1. Swipe down from the top of the screen to open the quick actions menu, and then tap **Settings**.
2. Tap on **Parental Controls**.
3. Then tap the switch next to **Parental controls**.
4. Enter a password of your choice.
5. To **disable parental controls** at any time, tap the switch again.
6. Tap on **Amazon Content and Apps** to restrict access to one or more of the following features:

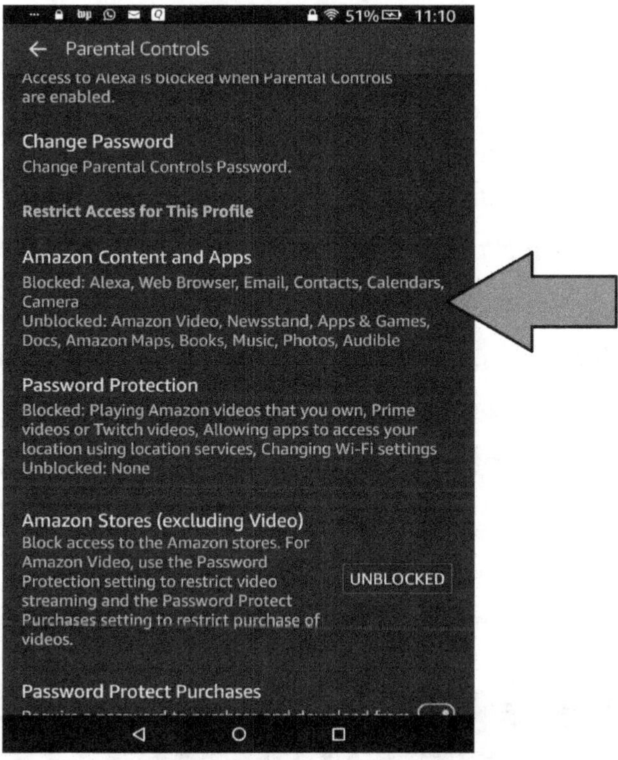

i. Web browser (Silk browser)

ii. Camera

iii. Social Networks

iv. Email and Calendar

v. The ability to play videos on Amazon Instant Video

vi. The ability to purchase content on your device

vii. Specific content types like books and audible

From the parental controls menu, you can also manage your child's profile, to do this, tap on the child's profile. You should see a padlock icon at the top of the screen when parental controls are active on your device.

Security

Allowing non-Amazon app installation

Allowing the installation applications from third parties or from stores other than Amazon appstore is very important when you want to get around the restriction posed by Amazon limited Appstore. By enabling this feature, you will be able to install many apps from stores other than Amazon.

1. Swipe down from the top of the screen to open the quick actions menu, and then tap **Settings**.
2. Tap on **Security & Privacy**.
3. Tap the switch next to **Apps from Unknown Sources**.

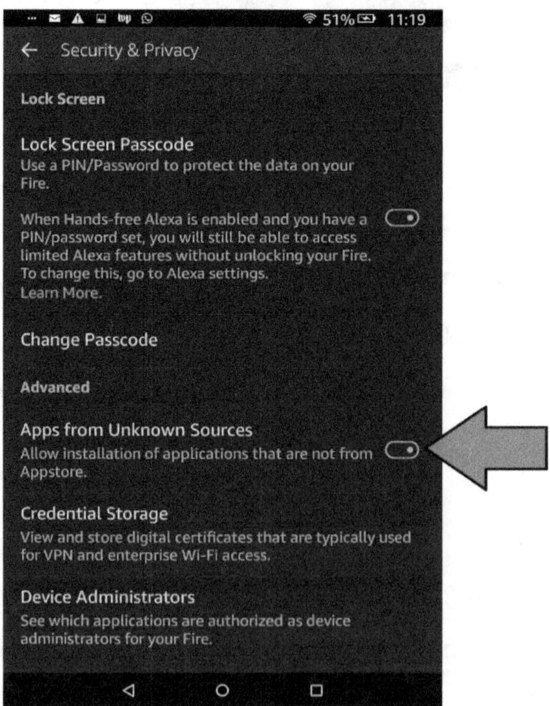

Note: We will advise that for security reason you turn this feature off whenever you are not using it, only turn it on when you want to install third parties app from a source other than Amazon.

Lock Screen

Please refer to page 23 to learn more.

Credential Storage

This allows you to access all stored digital certificates.

Device Administrators

This option allows you view which applications are authorized as device administrators for your Fire tablet.

Encryption

This option allows you to encrypt the internal storage of your Fire tablet.

Device Usage Data

Use this option to manage the data collected by the operating system of your device for marketing and product improvement.

Sounds & Notifications

This feature allows you to configure your sound and notification settings. Please refer to page 20 to learn more.

Keyboard & Language

Use this option to control the keyboard and language settings on your device.

Manage keyboard and Language

Please refer to the preceding section on *keyboard & language* (see page 17) to learn more.

Text-to-Speech

Use this option to manage the Text-to-Speech option.

Current Keyboard

Use this tab to change the current keyboard on your device to another one.

Show/Hide Keyboards

This tab allows you to tell your device which installed keyboards can be set as default.

Sync Device

Use this feature to sync your device so that it can receive content from the cloud and receive new software updates.

Help

Use this option to get help information on your device and also contact Amazon technical support.

Accessibility

This option allows you to manage accessibility features on your device, for more information on this, please refer to preceding chapter on *accessibility* (see page 93).

Legal & Compliance

This feature gives you information on privacy policies, safety & compliance, terms of use, and legal notices for your device.

What You Must Know About Your Fire Tablet

Removing Special Offers Banner

If you purchased a Fire Tablet with Special Offers, you will be charged a one-time payment to unsubscribe from the service.

To unsubscribe from Special Offers:

1. Launch www.amazon.com/mycd.
2. Click on **the Device** tab.
3. Click on the three dots icon next to your device name.
4. Next to **Special Offers/Offers and Ads,** click **Edit,** and then follow the onscreen instructions to unsubscribe from Special Offers.

How to take a screenshot on your device

Another task you can perform on your device is taking a screenshot. To take a screenshot with your device, please follow the instructions below:

1. Navigate to the required page (the page you want to take its screenshot).

2. Place one finger on the volume down button and the other finger on the power button and press these two buttons simultaneously.

3. To locate your screenshots, swipe down from the top of the screen. Alternatively, from the Home screen, tap **Amazon Photos**.

How to Find Your Tablet When lost

As a human being, it is possible you misplace your tablet. If someone else (a thief) has not taken custody of it, there are steps to follow in order to find it. These steps have been discussed at length in the preceding chapter; please refer to page 156 for details.

Amazon Limited App – You have little To Worry About

Amazon Fire tablet operates on Fire OS. This OS is a forked version of Android OS, i.e. Fire OS was built by making some changes to Android OS. Thus, many applications that normally work on Android OS will work on Fire OS.

However, considering the fact that Fire OS is not entirely similar to Android OS, you may still have some apps that are working on Android OS but will refuse to work on the Fire OS.

Anyway, many apps that work on Android OS will also work on Fire OS and you should be able to install many apps present on Google Play but not on Amazon Appstore by sideloading these apps on your tablet.

How to sideload an app on Amazon Fire Tablet

A. The first thing to do when sideloading an app is to change your settings so that your tablet can allow the installation of non-Amazon apps. You can follow the steps below:

1. Swipe down from the top of the screen to open the quick actions menu, and then tap **Settings**.
2. Tap on **Security & Privacy**.
3. Tap the switch next to **Apps from Unknown Sources**.

Note: We will advise that for security reason you turn this feature off whenever you are not using it, only turn it on when you want to install third parties app from a source other than Amazon.

B. Download and install this **ES File Explorer**. This app will enable you to easily locate any application file you download from the internet.

C. Download the APK file of the app you want to sideload. APK file can crudely be defined as the installation file of an app. When you have an APK file of an app, you can install the app on your device. To download the APK file of an app:

1. Go to play.google.com from your silk browser.
2. Search for the app of your choice in the store.
3. Then copy the address of the application from the address of bar of your silk browser.
4. Type apps.evozi.com/APK-downloader into the silk browser and launch it.
5. Then paste the address you copied in step 3 into the address bar found on the webpage.
6. Click on **Generate Download Link**
7. Then tap on **Click here to Download...**

8. If prompted to select an application to complete the downloading process, select Silk browser and follow onscreen instructions to complete the download.

D. Open the ES File Explorer App, and locate **Download** in the drop-down menu. This will show you the files you have downloaded on your tablet. Tap on the file of the app you want to install and then tap on install.

E. When you are done installing the app, go the app grid and look for the app you have just installed. With this method, you should be able to install as many as possible apps. Alternatively, you may first download the app APK to your PC, and then transfer it to your tablet using the USB cable.

To learn how to sideload Google Play store please refer to the bonus chapter on page 190.

Tip: You can also download the APK of an app by searching for the name of the app followed by APK. For example, you can search for **Files Go by Google APK**. Tap on a genuine website from the search results and follow the onscreen instructions to download the APK. After downloading the APK, tap on the APK file to install it on your device.

App Store to Consider

There are quite a number of app store to consider when using your Fire tablet. The one I will like to recommend is APKMirror. This website give you the ability to download the APK of an app. You can access APKMirror by visiting **https://www.apkmirror.com**

Simply go to this website and search for the app you want to download.

Note: Because of the risk of exposing yourself to malware, we will advise that you have antiviruses like *Lookout Antivirus* or *Mobile Security & Antivirus* on your tablet.

How to Access Google Drive And Other Cloud Drives Easily

There is a cool way to access Google Drive and other cloud drives without having to sideload their apps. You can follow the steps below to get this done.

1. Download **ES File Explorer** from Amazon Appstore and install it (you can skip this step if you have already done so).
2. Open the app and tap on **Cloud Drive**. If you can't see Cloud Drive, tap on **Network** and then **Cloud**.
3. Select **Log in to Google Drive** or **Log in with other cloud drive**, and then follow the onscreen instructions to complete the setup.

Solution to Non-Responding Apps

Sometimes an app may start misbehaving and may even refuse to close. The first thing you can do is to tap on the task-switcher button ▣ (the button besides the home button) to see all recently opened apps or items. Locate this particular app, and tap on **X** icon to close it.

Try launching the app again. If it is still misbehaving then you may follow these steps:

4. Swipe down from the top of the screen to open the quick actions menu, and then tap **Settings** ⚙.

5. Tap on **Apps & Games**.

6. Then tap on **Manage All Applications**.

7. Then tap on the misbehaving application from the list of applications.

8. Select **Force Stop**. This will stop the app from carrying out any process on your tablet. To enable the app again, just launch the app. Please note that it is usually unnecessary to force stop an app unless it is misbehaving.

You also have the option to clear data, clear cache, or clear default of the app. When you choose clear data, all the stored information like settings of the app will be lost but the app will not be uninstalled. This means that the next time you launch the app, you will be using it as if you are using it for the first time. When you choose clear cache, the cache memory is cleared. Cache is a set of data stored on a computer memory so that future requests for data can be served faster. The clear default allows you to clear any default setting you might have stored on the app.

How To conserve Fire Tablet's Battery Life

You may notice that you have to charge Fire tablet twice a day in order to keep your tablet on. There are steps to follow to ensure that your tablet serves you throughout the day with just a single charge.

1. **Reduce the screen brightness:** We have realized over time that screen brightness consumes a lot of energy. There is usually a substantial difference between using a tablet with maximum brightness and using it with moderate brightness. As a rule, don't use your tablet with a maximum brightness unless you can't see what is on the screen clearly, for example, if you are outdoor, and please make sure you reduce it immediately when it is no more needed.

2. **Shorten the Screen timeout:** If you really want to save your battery you must try to shorten the screen timeout (see page 164). Reducing how long your tablet will stay lit up after you finish interacting with it will help you to save battery.

3. **Turn off Wi-Fi and Bluetooth:** When you are not using Wi-Fi or Bluetooth please always remember to put them off. These features really consume energy and they are better off when not in use.

4. **Reduce the number of notifications:** There are two benefits of doing this, the first is that there will be less distractions and the second benefit is that notifications consume energy. Limit yourself to those notifications that are important to you. To learn how to disable notifications for individual app, please see page 20.

5. **Close all unnecessary apps:** Any opened app may be using out of the limited battery energy. It is important to close any app you are not using from time to time. To access all apps currently running on your tablet, tap on the task-switcher button ▣ (the button beside the home button). To close any of the opened apps, tap on **X** icon.

6. **Use a correct charger:** Using the wrong charger can endanger the health of your tablet/battery, and it is better to avoid such practice.

7. **Consider switching off your tablet:** If you are not going to use your tablet for an extended period, you may consider switching off your tablet.

8. **Go to the Power tab under your Fire tablet settings**: Power tab contains settings that can help you manage your battery life. To learn more about Power tab, see page 160.

9. **Use headphones:** Using headphones is another cool way to save your battery. Extended use of audio speakers of your tablet may drain your battery faster.

How to read EPUB on your device

You can read EPUB books using the OverDrive app. This is particularly cool since some books are in EPUB format and not in Kindle format.

If books through your local library system are not available on Kindle, they are usually in an EPUB format. This app makes getting and reading books in this format easy.

To download and install the OverDrive app, go to Amazon appstore. Download this app and follow the onscreen instructions to set it up. You can also buy **Aldiko Book Reader Premium** from Amazon App Store to read EPUB materials.

How to send personal document to your fire tablet or any Kindle device

One way to send personal documents to your device is through USB which we have already discussed on page 150-152. However, we will like to discuss another way to send personal document to your Fire tablet. This is through the use of **Send-to-Kindle E-mail.**

Send-to-Kindle E-mail is a unique address that is assigned to you when you register your compatible Fire tablet, Kindle e-reader or supported Kindle reading app.

The files supported on Send-to-Kindle include DOC, DOCX, HTML, PDF, TXT, GIF, RTF, JPEG, PNG, BMP, PRC, and MOBI. You can send any of your documents in the format mentioned above to your Kindle.

To view your Send-to-Kindle E-mail:

1. Swipe down from the top of the screen to open the quick actions menu, and then tap **Settings**.
2. Tap on **My Account**.
3. You will find the email address below your account name (found at the top of the screen). The email address usually ends with *kindle.com*.

Sending documents to your Send-to-Kindle E-mail address

To send a document to your Kindle device or app, simply attach it to an e-mail addressed to your Send-to-Kindle e-mail.

Notes:

- It is not necessary to include a subject in the email.
- The total size of the documents you want to send should be less than 50 MB and your email should not contain more than 25 attachments in order to avoid running into any problem.

- Amazon makes it possible to be able to add notes, highlights, and bookmarks to your personal documents. In addition, your notes, highlights, and bookmarks are synchronized across devices along with the last page read via Whispersync technology. Note that this synchronization feature is only available for personal documents archived in Kindle format. Interestingly, some documents formats are supported by the Amazon conversion service, but charges may apply.

Adding/Deleting an Approved Email Address

Documents can only be sent to your Kindle device from e-mail accounts that you have added to Approved Personal Document E-mail List.

To add/delete an approved e-mail address:

1. Launch www.amazon.com/mycd
2. Click on **Preferences** (or **Settings**) tab and scroll down to **Personal Document Settings**.
3. Under the **Approved Personal Document** E-mail **List**, click on **Add a new approved e-mail address**.
4. Enter the desired e-mail address and click **Add Address**.

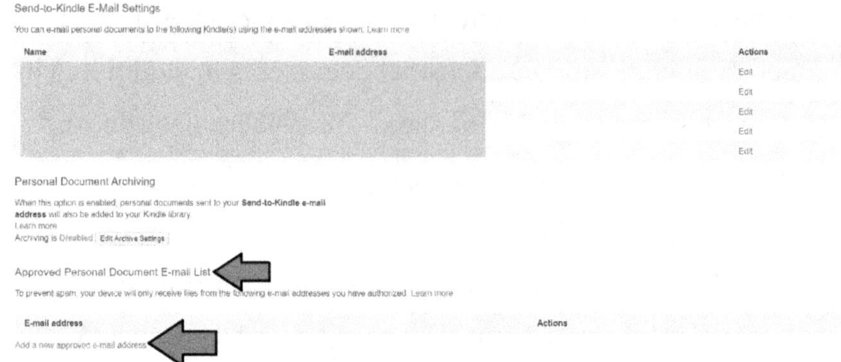

5. To remove an approved e-mail address, click on **Delete** next to the address you wish to remove.

Extras

Getting an antivirus for your tablet -- is it necessary?

Many people may not really take the issue of antivirus serious because they think that virus software target PC much more than tablets. The truth is that things are changing every now and then. The best thing you can do is to always keep a guard. There are many reputable free antiviruses on Amazon Appstore. My favorite antiviruses are AVG, Lookout and Mobile Security and Antivirus. You may search for these antiviruses on Amazon appstore.

Safety Precautions When Using Fire Tablet on Wi-Fi

With many free Wi-Fi hotspots, it is likely that you are going to find yourself using Wi-Fi more on your tablet. There are a few things to keep in mind when using Wi-Fi.

1. **Confirm the Network Name**

Hackers sometimes set up a fake Wi-Fi network in order to tap into the information of unwitting public users. To avoid this, make sure you are sure of the name of the network you are connecting to.

You may ask any trusted individual around you if you doubt the name of a network.

2. Connect To Secure Site

Whenever you are sending sensitive information always make sure that the site is a secure website. You can know whether a website is a secured site or not by checking whether the URL address of the website starts with **HTTPS.** If it starts with https, then it should be a secure site.

3. Run an Antivirus Software

As earlier mentioned, using an antivirus is very crucial in today's world. You may consider installing a genuine antivirus. Go to Amazon Appstore to download antivirus for your tablet.

4. Get a Virtual Private Network (VPN)

It is highly important you use a virtual private network when using a public network. There are both free and paid VPN providers. My favorite is Hotspot Shield VPN. It is available on Amazon Appstore. They offer both free and paid versions. You may also check out other VPN apps to pick the best.

5. Avoid Automatic Connection

Make sure your Wi-Fi is off when not using it to avoid your tablet automatically connecting to an open network. Turning your Wi-Fi off when not using it will also save your battery energy.

I am Having a Dwindling Love for my Fire Tablet; What Should I do?

It is possible that after buying a Fire tablet, you realize that it performs below your expectations. It is likely that you dislike your tablet because of its hardware or software issue. Generally, the hardware has to do with the design, the tablet makeup, the weight of the tablet, etc. while the software has to do with OS and applications. If your love for Fire Tablet is reducing because of the software; there is a way out. Although Amazon Appstore may not be robust enough, there are ways to sideload many great apps on your device. Sideloading great apps should transform your experience with your Fire tablet. It is likely that with the right apps, you may have little or no problem with your device. You can check page 176 to learn more about sideloading an app.

If your love for Fire tablet is reducing because of the hardware then it is either you learn how to live with it (you may have to force yourself to love it) or you sell it.

Bonus Chapter

How to Sideload Google Play Store on Fire Your Tablet

You can follow the steps below to sideload Google Play.

You will need *ES File Explorer* to complete this process and since we have mentioned this app several times, we will assume that you have already installed it, so we will not talk about its installation again.

1. Go to **https://forum.xda-developers.com/amazon-fire/general/how-to-install-google-play-store-fire-t3486603**
2. Download the four folders contained in the download link
3. Open **ES File Explorer** and locate the download folder. You may need to tap on **Internal Storage** found at the top of the screen to locate the download file.
4. Then tap on the APK files you have downloaded to install them in this order:

   i. Google Account Manager

   ii. Google Services Framework

   iii. Google Play Services

iv. Google Play Store

Notes:

- The order of installation of the various Google APKs has been found to be important, hence please make sure that you follow the correct order of installation so as to make sure you get the desired result.

- You may need to turn off Amazon store auto-update feature in order to preempt any errors.

- If you have not changed your settings to allow the installation of non-Amazon apps, then you will need to do so before you can install the four folders above. Please refer to page 170 to know how to change your settings.

- We cannot guarantee that this approach will continue to work, and we will advise that you use alternative apps store like APKMirror.com.

- Please if this approach does not work for you, try contacting us @ **pharmibrahimguides@gmail.com** or ajadirid1@gmail.com

Troubleshooting

If the touch screen responds slowly or improperly or your tablet is not responding, try the following:

- Remove any protective covers (screen protector) from the touch screen.
- Ensure that your hands are clean and dry when tapping.
- Press the power button once to lock the screen and press it again to unlock the screen and enter a PIN/password if required.
- Press and hold the **Power** button until your device restarts automatically.

Your Tablet Doesn't Charge

- Make sure you are using Amazon charger to charge your tablet.
- If the Fire tablet does not indicate that it is charging, unplug the power adapter and then switch off your tablet and switch it on again. Then plug back the charger.
- Make sure you are using the USB cable that came with the Fire tablet or anyone that has similar specs.

Forgot Lock Screen Password or PIN

1. Go to **www.amazon.com/mycd**
2. Go to **Devices** tab located at the upper center of the screen (if you are browsing with a desktop).
3. Click on the options tab next to the device you want to unlock.

4. Click on **Remote Lock**.

5. Enter and then confirm a new password or PIN, and then select **lock Device.**

6. Tap **Unlock** Device on your tablet and then enter the new password or PIN you just created and tap **OK.**

Alternatively:

1. From the lock screen on your device, enter a wrong password/PIN five times.

2. After the fifth incorrect attempt, a notification should appear with options.

3. Select **Reset Password** from these options.

4. Enter your Amazon account password and follow the prompts.

Your device is hot to the touch

When you use applications that require more power or use applications on your device for an extended period of time, your tablet may be a bit hot to touch. This is normal and it should not affect performance. You may just allow your tablet to rest for some time or close some applications.

Your tablet is not responding to touch

Make sure you have not accidentally turned On **VoiceView** (see page 93). If you have not, then try restarting your device.

Your tablet freezes or has a fatal error

If your tablet freezes or it is unresponsive, press and hold the power button until your switch off. Then press the power button to turn on your device again.

Tablet does not connect Wi-Fi

Make sure you don't have limited network connectivity in that area. If your network is good and you still cannot connect, you may perform any of these actions:

- Make sure your Airplane Mode is off.

- Try restarting the Wi-Fi settings.

- Move closer to your router and scan for the available networks. If the network still does not shows up, you may add the network manually.

- Restart your router and modem. Unplug the modem and router for few minutes and plug the modem in and then the router.

- Try restarting your tablet.

Another Bluetooth device is not located

- Ensure Bluetooth feature is activated on your tablet and the device you want to connect to.

- Ensure that your tablet and the other Bluetooth device are within the maximum Bluetooth range.

- Ensure that the device you are trying to connect with is having a supported Bluetooth profile. Please refer to the page 154-155 to find the list of supported Bluetooth profiles.

A connection is not established when you connect your tablet to a PC

- Ensure that the USB cable you are using is compatible with your device.

- Ensure that you have the proper drivers installed and updated on your PC.

Purchased content not showing

- Verify that your tablet is registered to the correct Amazon account. To confirm your registration, swipe down from the bottom of the screen and tap on settings ⚙. Tap on **My Account** and check the registered name. If you see a wrong account, tap **Deregister** and then register a new account.

Safety precautions

A. To prevent electric shock, fire, and explosion

1. Do not use damaged power cords or plugs, or loose electrical sockets.
2. Do not touch the power cord with a wet hand.
3. Do not bend or damage the power cord.
4. Do not short-circuit the charger.
5. Do not use your tablet during a thunderstorm.
6. Do not dispose of your tablet by putting it in fire.

B. Follow all safety warnings and regulations when using your device in restricted areas.

C. Comply with all safety warnings and regulations regarding mobile device usage while operating a vehicle.

D. Proper care and use of your tablet

1. Keep your tablet dry. Your tablet is not water-resistant.
2. Do not use or store your tablet in a very hot or cold areas.
3. Do not put your tablet near magnetic fields.
4. Do not use camera flash close to the eyes of people or pets because it can cause temporary loss of vision or damage the eyes.
5. When cleaning your tablet, do not use chemicals or detergents. You may use a small towel.
6. Keep your tablet away from small children because they may mistakenly damage it. It may look like a toy to them.

Just Before You Go (Please Read!)

Although we have put in tremendous effort into writing this guide,

We are confident that we have not said it all.

We have no doubt believing that we have not written everything possible about this device.

So we want you to do us a favor.

If you will like to know how to perform a task that is not included in this guide, please let us know by sending us an email at **ajadirid1@gmail.com** or **pharmibrahimguides@gmail.com**. We will try as much as possible to reply you as soon as we can.

Index